The Emotional Side of Men

JERRY SCHMIDT
AND
RAYMOND BROCK

HARVEST HOUSE PUBLISHERS
Eugene, Oregon 97402

THE EMOTIONAL SIDE OF MEN

Dedication

JERRY: To three men I love:
My dad, Art
My two sons, Cory and Ryan
And to my best friend: My wife, Karen, who has given me a deeper understanding of my emotions.

RAY: To two men who have deeply influenced my life:
My father, Clarence
My son, Robert
And to my wife, Lynita, who has encouraged me to explore the dimensions of Christian manhood.

Contents

Preface

Through the centuries questions concerning manhood and masculinity have been examined, debated, and repudiated. Each culture had defined the role of the male in society. But these definitions have been frequently revised.

The Athenian male of ancient Greece differed from his Spartan counterpart; the Roman soldier was different from the invading Goths. The knights of medieval Europe were different from the masters of the guilds, and the landholders from the serfs.

Today there is little uniformity in expectations placed on males. And the expectations change as the male grows older. Family roles, cultural expectations, and societal demands all impinge on the emerging male to the point of confusion, which leads too easily to an identity crisis, not only for men but also for women.

We believe that the Bible speaks consistently to manhood from a Christian perspective and defines what a man should be like in the closing decades of the twentieth century. Rather than being compelled to adopt the model portrayed by the mass media, we believe that men should be free to follow a higher order of expectations and principles. Developing masculinity from a Christian perspctive is a viable option. When masculinity is examined from a Biblical stance, it will lead to a lifestyle that is consistent with spiritual values and will permit the development of the full manhood potential created by God and illustrated through His Son, Jesus Christ.

It is our deepest desire that both men and women will pick up this book and read it from cover to cover. We have a male-female identity crisis going on today that we believe is partially responsible for such social problems as depression, divorce, homosexuality, and loneliness. Only through developing some clarity about what "maleness" seems to be and what it *ought* to be will male and and female be able to live in harmony, peace, and love.

We believe that it is within the divine order that men be permitted to be men of God and not feel threatened by a divergent model in the contemporary culture. It is to illustrate how we believe this can happen that we have collaborated on this book. We trust that its message will inspire men, young and old, to search the Scriptures and define for themselves what Christian manhood is all about, and to enjoy the full dimensions of their masculinity. We also believe that women who are interested in understanding and relating to men will benefit from what we have written.

—Jerry A. Schmidt
—Raymond T. Brock

Chapter 1
Man's Dilemma

It's 6:00 A.M. Mark Sullivan quickly turns off the clock radio beside his ear so as not to awaken his slumbering wife next to him. The kids are also still in the sack and won't be waking up for another half hour or so, when he will be rushing out the door. As Mark lies there for a moment he concentrates on all the chores that must be done at work that day. He will have to make several phone calls to the head office to check on the new account. Wednesday through Friday this week, just like last, he will fly to L.A. for a briefing of his field representatives. "Just can't take a chance on them muffing this eight-million-dollar deal." That means little time for the family this week. He thinks, "My wife goes to all these Bible studies and finds out what I'm supposed to be doing. Then she lays it on me. I've built a barn and two fences this summer just to keep away from that nagging tongue." Then she asks *me,* 'Why are you avoiding me?' "

"I'd better get up," Mark realizes. "Got an early breakfast meeting." Already he is in high gear and pretty fretful about the day. His doctor has warned Mark about his high blood pressure and his lack of exercise, but he's too busy to play racquetball with the boys or jog with the men at work this week. There's just so much to be done!

Mark arrives at work, having had little or no contact with his family. There are correspondence, executive meetings, giving directions, a martini lunch. During lunch Mark's thoughts wander between halfhearted attempts to be interested in the staff meeting: "Maybe next year I'll take a vacation. I know—I'll take flowers home to Judy. I'll get home early, start a fire and . . . I wonder how I'll do in the bowling league tomorrow night. I've just got to top Jim White's high game this time. What will my men think if I don't? I wonder if I'll get my next promotion. I probably should put in another Saturday morning, at least, to get more brownie points.''

In the afternoon, Mark gets a call from his wife just as he's getting ready for dictation with his new secretary. Judy is irritated. Now both of the kids have strep throat. "Why can't she handle her part of the deal at home? I don't have time for such little problems. I've got to bring home the bacon," he thinks.

Later in the day the big boss comes to town unannounced for a dinner meeting, and Mark thinks, "Guess I'll have to postpone shopping tonight with Judy."

Mark wonders, "When will I get the money for our hot water heater that's on the blink? Guess I'm just old money-bags." Then he makes the dreaded phone call home to advise Judy that instead of 5:30 P.M. he will be home around 8:00 P.M., after his dinner engagement with the boss. He apologizes to his son for having to miss the soccer game, chokes back some tears, pulls himself together, and rationalizes, "It's for the good of the family. I have no choice. What does Judy expect out of me, anyway? She always tells me to call if I'm going to be late. Then I call and she chews me out."

Mark goes out with his boss and secretary. He puts on a front all evening with the boss, but finds his secretary stimulating. She shares her concern about being divorced and trying to handle young children. She responds to Mark's advice. Mark arrives home around 9:30 P.M. and is greeted by a cold stare from his wife. He peeks in at his kids, now fast asleep, tries for sex with Judy, and for the fifth time in a row she refuses, mumbling something about "I guess that's all I'm good for." Mark finally wanders into the family room to watch the evening news. He falls asleep in his recliner and wakes up to an early-morning show. He has fleeting thoughts of the busy next day and thinks, "Maybe the secretary and I could have some lunch tomorrow. It's secretary's week, isn't it?"

Does this sound at all familiar? Have you ever been in Mark's shoes? How long will Mark's marriage last? How long will he live? What will happen to his children? What kinds of feelings are locked up inside him? How many of his real emotions does he reveal? Does he love his career? Are his needs being met?

Where is *your* life going, man? Are you running scared? Angry? Fed up with your role, your routine? What is a man supposed to be, anyway?

WHAT IS MAN?

Let's begin with some twentieth-century images of man and our own confusion concerning what we should be, how we are to act, and what we are to think about and feel.

According to J. H. Gagnon, physical strength and aggressiveness are the male traits that have traditionally selected man out for two activities: 1) hunting, fishing, and farming, and 2) face-to-face combat. Through thousands of years men have carried out these activities with great vigor, fortitutde, and skill. But now our world is different. In this country physical strength is relatively obsolete as an important male role requirement.[1]

Can you think of many jobs with the big three—money, power, status—that demand tremendous physical strength? And yet our literary characters paint the picture of a "macho" male. What of Clint Eastwood, James Bond, Burt Reynolds, and the now-mortal "Duke" himself? Such a male is rational, physically impressive, sexually potent, and often violent in the attainment of his goals. He certainly is not very tender, sensitive, or warm.

In such a world many men choose to carve out an identity of what is left of the traditional macho roles. These men define themselves as that which women are not.[2] Men know that women are entering the hunting, fishing, and fighting. At one Midwestern university the increase in female students in the professional schools of medicine, law, and business has increased 330 percent, 550 percent, and 450 percent from 1960 to 1976.[3] Traditional men sense only increased competition, with no new options for themselves.

Thus we are caught. What used to be the sources for our self-esteem as men are being challenged and gradually eroded by the women's movement and changing social roles. Perhaps this is true because we have put all our eggs of self-worth in a few baskets. A man can feel good if he's sexually potent, aggressive, decisive, a leader, logical, a fighter, tough, objective, dominant, self-reliant, and angry. But so now can a woman! But if a man is tender, emotional, sensitive, indecisive, passive, compassionate, dependent, open, and vulnerable he is deemed *not* a man. Yet a woman can have these characteristics as well as the others and still be a woman! So we have denied ourselves many of the sources of self-esteem that women are now able to legitimately claim. Myron Brenton has stated: "As long as men feel that the equality of women will emasculate them, it is exactly what will happen. As long as men identify themselves so narrowly with the breadwinning role, with the competitive demands of their consumer society, with narrow and noncreative work, their psychic equilibrium will be shaky."[4]

In his insightful yet disturbing book *The Hazards of Being Male,* Herb Goldberg has said:

Deep inside a man knows that his attractiveness to a woman is closely linked to his continuing ability to succeed in the outside world. He knows that if he loses status, power or money he stands to lose sexual attractiveness and love as well. The male thus finds himself in an impossible bind. If he continues to pursue success vigorously he has less capacity for involvement in his love relationship. If he does not pursue vigorously, he becomes less desirable.[5]

Goldberg is not just engaged in "armchair philosophy" here. Weekly I seen men in counseling who verbalize being caught in the same trap Goldberg is alluding to: "I want to speak out and express my feelings, to spend more time with the family," they say, "but when I do, we can't pay the bills, and when I try to express my feelings my wife analyzes them and digs for more. When is she going to be satisfied with my efforts? I'm doing all I can. I'm almost burned out, *completely!*"

Women, then, must share the responsibility for helping put men in their stereotyped roles, just as men can share in the responsibility of some of women's trappings.

DESTRUCTIVE CONSEQUENCES

In this context, men are more vulnerable than are women to sudden, unpredictable behavior, such as drinking binges, wild driving, destructive affairs, and violent outbursts. At times a man can drive those close to him "crazy." First, his intimates take his controlled attitude at face value and assume that everything is okay. But then he himself comes to the conclusion that "no one really cares about me" and "to hell with them all! Don't they know how much I'm hurting, how hard I work?"

His repressed feelings are turned inward for so long that he is left lonely. He withdraws and is prone to depression, anxiety, and psychophysiological disorders. A man then alienates himself from relationships. He is lonely, numb, feeling futile. He may turn to alcohol, drugs, and shallow sexual relationships that reach no further than to give emotional release to pent-up feelings and ego needs.

Along with this, men tend to deny and tune out body signals of disease. When a man finally ends up in a hospital he stays 15 percent longer than a female. The death rolls for men offer these statistics:

1. Men are four to five times more likely to die from

       bronchitis, emphysema, and asthma than are women.
2. Death from cardiovasular diseases and cirrhosis of the liver occur twice as often among men.
3. Men die from hypertension 40 percent more often; pneumonia and influenza, 64 percent more often; arteriosclerosis, 20 percent more often; tuberculosis, 150 percent more often; and cancer, 40 percent more often.
4. For divorced males the death rate is 3.16 times higher for men than for women.

These facts are alarming. They say something about the quality of life of the man in our society. Wagenvoord and Bailey have summarized it well:

If he wants to be a man, then:

    He shall not cry
    He shall not display weakness
    He shall not need affection or gentleness or warmth
    He shall comfort but not desire comforting
    He shall be needed but not need
    He shall touch but not be touched
    He shall be steel and not flesh
    He shall not be inviolated in his manhood
    He shall stand alone.[6]

As men we live in prisons of loneliness, competition, and perfectionism. We are expected to be cool, calm, strong, and unemotional. We are islands, sexual conquerors. And since a man's greatest fear is probably *the fear of failure,* we work very hard at remaining in our prisons. These prisons are designed to defend us against any sign of weakness or inadequacy.

If we do not compete and win, we have failed. If we do not remain calm, cool, and strong in a crisis, we have failed. Certainly, if we do not have a woman who responds willfully and with passion in the bedroom, we have failed. And we must certainly never ask for help, lest someone think we are weak or incapable.

And what about touch? Can I touch another man without being accused of having latent homosexual urges? Can I touch a woman without being accused of holding lust in my heart? I am absolutely filled with pride when others see my father and me embracing as we greet one another or reluctantly say goodbye. What a freedom and a healing sensation touch can give to another person! What healing you can receive through touch!

Christian Marriage Encounter utilized a meaningful slogan: "Touch me and heal my anger." There's much truth to that statement. Yet we choose to not make contact, because it might be sinful or others might get the wrong idea. Or we might be labeled "sissy" or "strange" or "feminine" or. . . .

So, where are we going, men? We have weaknesses, true. We possess blind spots and we struggle with out own identity. Do we have any handles? Any positive guidelines, directions? Where can we go for help? Should we change because women's lib says so or because men's lib says so? Can we keep some of our masculine characteristics and still hold our heads up? Do we have to become sissies in order to conform to the new trends in what a man should be? Let's move on to the ensuing chapters and find some light that will help answer these questions.

Notes

1. J. H. Gagnon, "Physical Strength, Once of Significance," in D. S. David and R. Brannon, eds., *The Forty-nine Percent Majority: The Male Sex Role* (Reading, MA: Addison-Wesley, 1976).

2. Thomas Skouholt, "Feminism and Men's Lives," in *The Counseling Psychologist,* vol. 7, no. 4, 1978, pp. 3-9.

3. B. Hutter, "Feminist Caucus Issues Outlines," in *The Minnesota Daily,* Jan. 1978, p. 4.

4. Myron Brenton, *The American Male* (New York:

Coward-McCann, Inc., 1966).

5. Herb Goldberg, *The Hazards of Being Male* (New York: Signet, 1976), p. 35.

6. James Wagenvoord and Peyton Bailey, *Men: A Book for Women* (New York: Avon Books, 1978), p. 165.

Chapter 2
God's Perspective

Stepping out of the car at our mountain cabin, nestled in the trees of the Rockies, I gazed with awe into the heavens. All around was a picture of the firmament never seen in the city. The sky was filled with visible stars and planets. It was like gazing through a powerful telescope and seeing a detailed portrait of the universe. There were not words at that moment to describe my feelings. David, in Psalm 8, expressed in finite words, understandable to man, what some of these feelings were:

> O Lord our God, the majesty and glory of your name fills all the earth and overflows the heavens. . . . When I look up into the night skies and see the work of your fingers—the moon and the stars you have made—I cannot understand how you can bother with mere puny man, to pay any attention to him! (Psalm 8:1,3,4 TLB).

Leslie Brandt has paraphrased this Psalm and captured my feelings as I contemplated the heavens:

> When I gaze into star-studded skies
>   And attempt to comprehend the vast distances,
> I contemplate in utter amazement
>   my Creator's concern for me.
> I am dumbfounded that You
>   should care personally about me.
>
> And yet You have made me in Your image.
> You have called me Your son.
> You have ordained me as Your priest
>   and chosen me to be Your servant.

You have assigned to me the fantastic responsibility
of carrying on Your creative activity.

O God,
how full of wonder and splendor You are![1]

Let's paint an even clearer picture of God's power, His
concern for us, and how we need not feel insignificant in His
sight. We'll begin painting this picture by taking an imaginary trip through outer space. Let's travel at the speed of
light, 186,000 miles per second. That's 669,000,000 miles per
hour! If I were to stand stationary at this moment and fire a
bullet at the speed, the bullet would dart around the earth
and strike me in the back of my head 7½ times before normal reaction time would allow me to move out of the way!
That's fast! Let's jump into our spaceship, then, and blast
off at the speed of light. Our destination is to reach the back
side of our galaxy.

In about 15 minutes we've passed the sun, and we figure
that at this rate the trip will take no time, and that we'll probably be back in time for coffee break. But then we travel for a
day and we still haven't reached the back side of our galaxy.
We travel 2 days, 5 days, 10 days, 30 days. Still not there. We
speed on for another month, 6 months, a year, 5 years, 10
years, 20 years, 50, 100, 1000 years. One thousand years at
669,000,000 miles per hour and we still have not reached the
outer edge of our *own* galaxy! We speed on for 5000 years,
10,000, 20,000 years. We're starting to miss our families and
friends! We speed on for 30,000, 40,000, 50,000, 60,000
years. Finally, traveling at the speed of light for 60,000 years,
we reach the outer edge of our galaxy! Then some wise guy in
our spaceship says, "That wasn't so bad. Let's try the next
galaxy." But zipping along at this same speed of light, it
would take us one million more years to reach the *next-
closest* galaxy! *Within the bowl of the Big Dipper alone there
are a million galaxies!*

And then we hear the prophet Isaiah describing, again, in finite terms, who his God is:

> With whom will you compare me? Who is my equal? asks the Holy One. Look up into the heavens! Who created all these stars? As a shepherd leads his sheep, calling each by its pet name, and counts them to see that none are lost or strayed, so God does with stars and planets! (Isaiah 40:25,26 TLB).

Astronomers give us support for David's statement by indicating that they can predict the precise arrival of the stars and planets at a given point in space within *seconds* of their arrival, *and they do arrive precisely on time.* That's power! That's true omnipotence! Our Lord is the Shepherd of the stars. He could put *Star Wars* to shame. He travels in seconds among the vast distances we traveled a moment ago for 60,000 years at the speed of light! We cannot begin to fathom His power. Yet we have the audacity to question whether God has control, whether He is sovereign, whether He is *our* Shepherd.

Isaiah expands on this idea in Isaiah 40:27-31:

> O Jacob, O Israel, how can you say that the Lord doesn't see your troubles and isn't being fair? Don't you yet understand? Don't you know by now that the everlasting God, the Creator of the farthest part of the earth, never grows faint or weary? No one can fathom the depths of his understanding. He gives power to the tired and worn out, and strength to the weak. Even the youths shall be exhausted, and the young men will all give up. But they that wait upon the Lord shall renew their strength. They shall mount up with wings like eagles; they shall run and not be weary; they shall walk and not faint (TLB).

What a passage! If God is the Shepherd of the stars, of the vastness of the universe, if He has control over a trillion galaxies that would take humans an infinity of time and energy to explore, He is also *our* Shepherd. And it is an insult to God to doubt whether He has enough power to help us. It's actually a pretty humorous question to ask, isn't it? It certainly is a relief to know that God has a sense of humor.

God places us above the stars and heavens in importance. Within this context we certainly do not need to feel unimportant, low in self-esteem. We are worthy as men because the Shepherd of the stars says so. Do you wish to argue with the Shepherd of the stars? I'd rather argue with Darth Vader!

From this basis of being O.K. in God's sight we are free to move on toward perfection. Notice, I said *toward*. Psalm 37:23,24 states: "He delights in each step they take. If they fall it isn't fatal, for the Lord holds them with his hand" (TLB). And Paul in his letter to the Christians in Philippi says that he "presses on toward the mark, not looking back." He is saying that we do not have to blame ourselves continually for missing the mark in the past, but *instead* we are to press on, to keep trying, "walking steadily along God's pathway."

Let's look at some specific guidelines which men are to follow along God's pathway—some valid points of identity. We will begin with a study of the qualifications for elders in the early Christian church in Titus, as written to Timothy by Paul.

THE MEASURE OF A MAN

In Titus and I Timothy, Paul describes some critical criteria for elders of the early Christian church. Remember that these are goals we need to be shooting for, and are not meant to induce strong guilt. But if they produce just enough guilt or concern to get us off dead center and moving toward "the mark," we'll be satisfied.

Manhood Begins at Home

Titus 1:6-9 gives a list of qualifications for a church

elder. One thing is especially stressed in this list: the elder must be a man who has taught and trained his own family in the faith. Christianity begins at home. It is no virtue for any man or woman to be so engaged in public work that he or she neglects his or her home.[2]

In Psalm 101:2 David responds to prayers offered on his behalf at his coronation: "I will try to walk a blameless path, but how I need your help, especially in my own home, where I long to act as I should" (TLB). As men we are instructed to spend *time* with our family. And we are not to just *be with* them, but also to instruct them. One of the ways we can teach is through the model of our lives. As Gordon McDonald has said in *The Effective Father,* "If I am an effective father it is because I have devoted myself to become an instrument and model of human experience to my children."[3]

This means that if we are telling our children how important it is that they control their tempers, then we need to be working on the control of our own outbursts of destructive anger. If we are exhorting our children or our spouse to be more friendly toward other people, then we must watch our own expressions of friendliness and hospitality.

A second way that we can teach in the home is through actual verbal instruction. And this is to be done on a continual basis, according to Moses:

> And these words which I command you this day shall be upon your heart; and you shall *teach* them diligently to your children, and shall *talk* of them when you *sit* in your house, and when you *walk* by the way, and when you *lie* down, and when you *rise* (Deuteronomy 6:6,7 RSV).

We are to seize every opportunity of actual life experience to teach the principles of the Christian faith. As a father, take advantage of bedtime with your children. At our house, as often as possible, I put our boys to bed. This gives me a chance to talk with them about events of the day, relating them relevantly to our faith. Recently Cory, our oldest, was asking some rather significant questions concerning the reality of God, because of a negative experience he had had that day. I related to him that God doesn't always keep us from having negative experiences, but that He is there to help us deal and learn from them. Then we moved into a brief discussion concerning what Cory had learned from his fiasco. And he came to a new understanding of God's wisdom! Using real-life experiences to talk about and teach our Christian faith is an exciting way to be a man and a leader in the family.

The basis for manhood begins at home, as a *model* of decent, upright behavior and as an *instructor*.

A Man Must Be of Blameless Reputation

In I Timothy 3:1-7, Paul begins his list of what elders of the church are to be like. He begins by saying that a pastor must be a man of blameless reputation. In the RSV translation, the man must be "above reproach." This is a man whom no one can gossip about in a negative fashion. That's quite a challenge. To be above reproach means to be "above censure," "above any reprimand or dishonor." That means living as clean and moral a life as is humanly possible. If we are chosen, as man, to be models for others, this particular guideline makes a lot of sense. Do you know men about whom it is difficult to find negative statements or opinions? What are these men like? How do they live their lives? Apparently Paul had this kind of man in mind.

He Must Be Married to One Wife Only

Presently we have the highest divorce rate ever known. Only about 50 percent of modern-day marriages actually last! Paul exhorts Christian men to be loyal husbands. Even when you hit the midlife crisis and life seems to be passing you by, you are still asked to stick by your wife. Even though you no longer feel young and vibrant, and some sweet young thing comes along and builds you up to be a king, you are to cling to your wife. And even though you feel taken advantage of, that all you're good for is to "bring home the bacon" but are unappreciated by your family, you are asked to loyal to your wife. That's tough these days!

All around you friends and relatives are flying the coop for "happiness," and many are convinced they will find it in the next relationship. However, statistics show that second marriages are no more successful than first marriages. The chances for "happiness" in a second marriage are no better and actually somewhat less than in the first marriage.

During Paul's day, divorce was becoming rather commonplace. In Jewish law, grounds for divorce were infidelity, incompatability, and cruelty. The attitude was that it was far better to divorce and start over in the face of adversity. It sounds like commitment was not too fashionable in Paul's day, just as it is not today. I believe we are presently in the throes of rejecting intimacy, yet hoping that we can have a close relationship *without commitment*. Today "commitment if it's convenient," is the idea rather than saying, "I'll be committed regardless." That's tragic. Love is not just a feeling, a sexual urge, or a moment of romantic delight. It is unconditional commitment to an imperfect person.

He Must Be a Man of Self-Control and Discretion

Paul goes on to say that a man must be a person of "self-control and discretion." This refers to *keeping one's mind safe and sound*. My physiologist colleagues inform me that sensations and perceptions reach the *thinking* centers of the brain before they reach the emotional centers. It follows that we *think* before we feel and act. If you could put all your thoughts up on a giant theater screen, what would they look like? Would most of them be upright, positive, and uplifting? Would they reflect faith, hope, and love? Or would they reflect fear, doubt, and hate? In Proverbs we are reminded, "As a man thinks in his heart, so is he.'' There is a way of thinking which destroys and a way which saves. Which way are you going? What do you like about each day? What does your "screen" look like?

He Must Be a Man of Disciplined Life

A man is to be in control of his destructive emotions. This is not the same as suppressing emotions, but instead implies that a man is to *think* before acting. This means that if one of my boys is misbehaving, instead of thinking "revenge" it is better for me to be thinking, "My purpose is to teach, not punish." That mere thought has kept me at times from uttering cruel, destructive, crushing words at my sons, and has prodded me to utilize natural consequences, positive reinforcement, "I messages," and several other more-constructive strategies of discipline.

Leading a disciplined life also connotes that I am not to be impulsive. In other words, instead of blurting out the first thought that comes to mind, I am to stop and think how to state my feelings. Instead of impulsively buying a particular automobile or stock or piece of land or new camera, I am to shop around, list pros and cons, consider the consequences, and then make my decision. It's not that we should deny ourselves the legitimate pleasures of life, but that we should do some planning before we act.

Implied in a self-disciplined life is *organization*. Instead of letting the tax records heap up in a pile somewhere in the basement, we are called to keep good records so that we don't have to be in a complete panic when April 15 rolls around. Paul is saying that there is real strength to being somewhat methodical and organized. That's a "masculine trait" that is sometimes put down as being too staid and not living dangerously enough. Yet where would business, finance, institutions, and families be today without some organization, some routine, some purposeful planning and goal-setting? Donald Campbell said it well in his very helpful book, *If You Don't Know Where You're Going You'll End Up Somewhere Else.*

He Must Be Hospitable

In this passage in I Timothy, Paul says that a man should welcome other brothers into his house. And who is my brother? I wish I had a nickel for the number of times I have heard a woman say that it pleases her beyond words to see her husband, son, or male friend welcome other people to their home in a warm, friendly fashion. I know that this is something my wife has been very grateful about in our marriage. I haven't always lived up to being friendly and hospitable to guests, perhaps because I'm a bit reserved. But when I've made a second effort to be cordial, hospitable, and gracious, I know that she has appreciated it.

This implies an open heart, unselfishness, an "open house" philosophy. I believe that it is up to a man to set the atmosphere or feeling tone in a house. If this is so, being hospitable strikes me as critical. Here again, men are a model for the rest of the family as to whether they will make that second effort to be kind and gracious to other people. This may mean offering your dinner table to another person while his or her spouse is out of town on business or attending to a sick relative. Open your house and your heart.

A Man Must Have the Gift of Teaching

The finest and most effective teaching is not done by *speaking* but by *being*. Enough said.

He Must Not Be a Man Who Assaults Others

This means not assaulting physically or verbally. We can certainly damage others with out words:

"Any moron could figure that out!"
"If I've told you once, I've told you a thousand times, idiot!"
"You just can't learn anything, can you?"

"You're just plain frigid!"
"You are incredibly clumsy!"
"You're just like your mother!"

And the list could go on. We already wield enough power just being male without adding to that advantage by putting others down.

The fact is that fault-finding is the least effective tool we can use to motivate another human being. The fault-finder is hated, mistrusted, and feared. You really are not teaching anything constructive through fault-finding. How does calling your son a moron help him achieve in school? How does calling your wife frigid help her respond to you sexually.?

He Must Be Gentle

This means that we are to pardon human failings. We are to look to the intention, not only the action. If your child is trying to do a good job but doesn't succeed to the level you had determined he should, reinforce him for trying, for putting forth effort. This is focusing on the positive rather than on evil or the negative.

James 3:17 further describes this gentle spirit:

But the wisdom that comes from heaven is first of all pure and full of quiet gentleness. Then it is peace-loving and courteous. It allows discussion and is willing to yield to others; it is full of mercy and good deeds. It is wholehearted and straightforward and sincere (TLB).

In her excellent book *Tough and Tender,* Joyce Landorf suggests that there are 11 words which have to do with being a "gentle" man. She suggests that you mentally score yourself as to when these words become actions with your wife or children. It is a way to evaluate your *tender* abilities. The words are:[4]

1. Consideration
2. Sympathy
3. Helpfulness

7. Unselfishness
8. Politeness
9. Understanding

4. Tact
5. Courtesy
6. Compassion

10. Thoughtfulness
11. Social manners

If you can say yes to six or seven of these adjectives being true of you, you probably have a very special relationship going at your house. Your wife is deeply in love with you, and vice versa. If your score is three or less, there are probably some large gaps in your understanding of each other. And your home is probably a rather cold and uncomfortable place to live. It may also be revealing to have your wife and children go through this checklist and give their perceptions of you as well.

The real gentleman, then, is interested in what he can do to make his family happy—what he can *give,* not *take.*

A Man Must Be Peaceable

We are advised here not to be "trigger-happy," ready to blow up at any instant. We are asked to be disinclined to fight. Instead of serving as an angry model for our children and blowing up at the neighbors, we are to approach them with our gripes and complaints in an attitude of peace.

In Titus 1:7 this characteristic of a man is reinforced: he must not be an angry man. Here Paul is talking especially about "ogre" anger. This kind of anger is inveterate, the wrath a man nurses to keep it warm. It's like keeping a gunnysack full of little irritations and almost delighting in keeping your anger inside so that you'll have good reason to blast away at a moment's notice. The only problem is that *people* get blasted away.

He Must Be Free from the Love of Money

Jesus said that it would be harder for a rich man to enter the kingdom of God than it would be for a camel to enter through the eye of a needle! When we love money and its procurement more than people, we're in trouble, because it means working 70-hour weeks, getting ulcers over "how to invest," evading income tax, stepping on people on our way up, manipulating other people, and scores of other dehumanizing actions.

He Must Not Be Obstinately Self-willed

A man is not to please himself only. A self-willed man cares to please no one. He obstinately maintains his own opinion or declares his own right while being reckless of the rights, opinions, and interests of other people. This same kind of man is intolerant, and condemns everything that he does not understand.

In Titus 1:7 Paul is asking that men be assertive in the sense of allowing others their opinions, rights, and interests. A man is allowed his right to ask for what he needs, but he is also instructed to allow other people to have their own feelings and attitudes without condemning them. How does that translate into the way we are to treat our workmates, employees, bosses, friends, acquaintances, sons, daughters, and wives? It means that we allow others their individuality.

If your teenage daughter holds a particular opinion about whether a woman must marry or bear children and you happen to disagree, how should this be handled? We are instructed here to encourage the daughter to express her opinion. We are not to jump down her throat and condemn her if she does not agree, even though we are convinced that we hold a more wholesome view! Certainly, as a man and father, you can share *your* opinions just as she has hers. But it is my opinion that you will earn more of that daughter's respect and love by allowing her to hold that opinion than by putting her down and telling her that she is not thinking clearly.

A Man Must Be Able to Encourage Others

There is always something wrong with a religion and with preaching and teaching that discourages people. We are told in Scripture not to provoke our children to wrath lest we discourage them. The function of the true Christian man is not to drive someone else to despair, but to lift him or her up to hope. And how do we give another person hope? By encouraging that person, by supporting him or her. In giving positive feedback and sharing our own blind spots with other people, we give them hope and assurance that they are not alone in the struggle of life. By knocking out overpiousness and snobbishness in our faith, we offer hope to fellow strugglers. Someone once said, "Be kind to every person you meet; he is having a hard time." How true!

He Must Be Able to Convict the Opponents of the Faith

As men we are called to share the meaning that our relationship with God brings to our lives. This does *not* mean that we shove our faith down someone else's throat. It *does* mean that we should feel free, when the time is right, to share what our faith means to us, how it works in our lives. This is an important way of offering another person hope. Recently a man in midlife asked me what I thought of religion. I asked him if he really wanted to know. When he assented, I shared with him the extent and depth of my own convictions regarding my relationship with my Lord. Apparently this man became convinced that what I was talking about was real and was working tangibly in my life. He accepted the Lord that day, not because I had browbeaten him into believing, but merely because I shared with him my own experiences and convictions.

Somehow we have bought the idea that if I believe in God, I am weak, a sissy! Where did we get that idea? Perhaps in part it comes from a female-dominated church or from the idea among some people that Jesus was effeminate. Perhaps another reason is that somehow believing is thought not to be based upon logic, but upon an emotional response. And we know how we males respond to anything that smacks of emotionalism. We run and hide from it; we become dubious and hold a "healthy doubtfulness." We distance ourselves from stepping out in faith by getting into rational discussions about religion. So what's wrong with *experiencing* God's love in an emotional way and expressing it?

The way we witness to our faith is by sharing what we *experience* as a result of our relationship with God. Certainly we will not influence another man toward our faith by telling him what a terrible sinner he is. Nor will we have any influence by remaining passive and not speaking about God, as if He were a taboo topic. We can share what works in our lives. There's nothing that appeals more to another man than the pragmatic. Share your faith and how it is *practical* for you.

Notes

1. Leslie Brandt, *Psalms Now* (St. Louis: Concordia, 1973), p. 17.
2. William Barclay, *The Letters to Timothy, Titus, and Philemon* (Philadelphia: The Westminster Press, 1960).
3. Gordon McDonald, *The Effective Father* (Wheaton: Tyndale House, 1977).
4. Joyce Landorf, *Tough and Tender* (Old Tappan, NJ: Fleming H. Revell, 1975).

Chapter 3
Loneliness Versus Developing Relationships

Kyle sat dejectedly across from me and stared at the floor in my office. Interspersed between long pauses he spun a tale of loneliness that dated from early childhood. Although he had several brothers and sisters, he had never felt like he fit into the family. His relationship with his mother was strained, and his relationship with his father was almost nonexistent.

He had not dated in high school and very little in college. All of his attempts at forming friendships, both male and female, had met with utter disaster. On the surface he remained aloof and pretended he didn't care, but inside he was hurting enough to initiate counseling.

His job as an insurance adjuster was driving Kyle up the wall. He could do his write-ups once he had made his assessments, but he could not bring himself to face his clients and gather the information needed to settle their claims. No matter where he was—in the office, at home, or at church—Kyle felt isolated. At night he filled his apartment with the sounds of TV or stereo to break the silence as he ate the fast-food meals he picked up on his way from work. Only his regular routine of jogging brought any sense of satisfaction into his life, but he went out early so there would be no one else on the track that circled the park across from his apartment complex.

Kyle is not alone in his loneliness. It is the obvious plight of many single, divorced, and widowed individuals, and it is a specter lurking in the shadows of many marriages as well.

Loneliness was the first emotion man ever had that he

could not handle. Loneliness is a part of the human condition. It is not something to be learned: it is innate; it pervades the universe. Loneliness comes into life from a variety of sources, but all human beings experience loneliness to varying degrees at various stages of life.

ORIGINS OF LONELINESS

Behavioral scientists have come up with a variety of approaches to the origin of loneliness. No single cause fits every case, but each idea sheds light on a universal problem.

Childhood Beginnings

The roots of loneliness may lie in childhood. Sigmund Freud used the term *megalomania* to describe the infantile feelings of impotence, power, and importance that a child learns while he is dependent on others for survival. He learns that by a simple cry he can be fed, changed, held, fondled, or cuddled. His every need is met if he just lets out a whimper or cry of distress.

Some people never outgrow the temptation to hang on to such dependence. When they become adult and revert to childish behavior, they experience rejection. Rejection leads to feelings of isolation, which deepens into depression.

Freud drew on Greek mythology to illustrate the point. As a youth, Narcissus saw his reflection in a quiet pool. He became so enamored with his own beauty that he spent a lifetime just admiring his reflection in the water. Life passed him by. Narcissism, neurotic self-love, becomes the temptation of the man who has not been able to disengage from the power struggles of infancy and childhood. Instead, he makes a lifetime occupation of tending to his own selfish needs.

When his is not successful through passive means, he then resorts to aggression and hostility. Sometimes this aggression is turned out on the world in acts of violence. Sometimes it is turned in on self in varying degrees of self-destruction. Miserable is the man who sees his every move toward acceptance blocked by a distorted view of himself and has to bludgeon his way through life to have his own way at any cost.

More vicious than attacks on others is the temptation of a man to turn anger in on himself. He becomes his own worst enemy and settles for mediocrity rather than exploring the dimensions of his inner self to fulfill his God-given potential. The rising rate of male suicide and of admissions to mental hospitals reflects the futility of inward aggression that leaves a man impotent in all areas of his life.

Faulty Communication

Another source of loneliness is faulty communication. The child who feels unloved—whether in reality or fantasy—leads a lonely adult life. Anxiety grows through a lack of self-acceptance, which is followed by feelings of rejection.

David Riesman says that lonely people are "other-directed."[1] They wait for someone to tell them what to do. Rather than making their own decisions, they turn to other people to solve their problems or give them suggestions. Then they follow the crowd in their loneliness, drifting through life as a ship without a rudder. They are so intent on seeking the approval of other people that they never really get around to doing what is important to them. Their source of direction rests in others, so their contemporaries manipulate them as pawns on a chessboard.

Fear

Loneliness can also result from fear. As Paul Tournier has observed, "Fear breeds loneliness and conflict." But it is also true that "loneliness and conflict breed fear."[2] So man is caught in a vicious cycle, lacking the courage to become what he was created by God to be.

Cosmic Discouragement

Looking into outer space with the naked eye is a challenge,

but a look at the universe through a telescope makes man feel even more insignificant. A significant source of loneliness can be cosmic discouragement, the conviction of insignificance that comes when man compares himself with the gigantic universe around him. Man's finiteness becomes oppressive when the crushing size of the universe threatens his role in the cosmic order, and it only aggravates his feelings of inadequacy. So man is caught in a paradox: getting caught up in a dilemma of estrangement from the universe or being so submerged in collective, suffering absorption that identity is lost in trying to forget the immensity of the universe.

Changing Pace of Change

Loneliness can also come from the changing pace of change. Change demands adjustment. The inability to adjust to the changing pace of change can lead to disorientation. When traditions are challenged and institutions questioned, it is tempting to give up and say, "What's the use?" But to do so is an exercise in futility, for as long as there is life there is challenge. When man ceases to face challenge creatively, he is already dead.

Alienation

Alienation is an advanced form of loneliness. When alienation creeps in on a man he perceives himself as a victim of circumstances beyond his control. The cold objectivity of science and technology only confirm man's loneliness and make him feel the futility of existence. There are basically five dimensions of alienation:

1. *Powerlessness.* This is the belief that one's own behavior cannot significantly determine the outcomes of life or bring realization of the goals he seeks. Since the person has no power over what is happening to him, apathy and surrender seem less frustrating. Emotional suicide leads to physical suicide and becomes what the youth culture calls a "cop-out."

2. *Meaninglessness*. Viktor Frankl has pointed out that a basic challenge for everyone is the search for meaning.[3] Rather than enter on this quest, the alienated male lacks understanding of the events in which he is engaged. He is uncertain as to what he believes or why. This leads to a low expectancy that there can be any rhyme or reason in his life, and the conclusion that it is useless to predict any consequences to his behavior. This attitude was prevalent among the hedonistic Greeks, who said, "Eat, drink, and be merry, for tomorrow we die."

3. *Normlessness*. Life demands a measure for its significance. Normlessness is the absence of spiritual or social guidelines against which to measure the effectiveness of life. Since the normal personality needs regulations and structure for behavior—a criterion against which to measure effective behavior—it is essential to come to grips with what is meaningful, not only for time, but also for eternity.

4. *Isolation*. Intellectual isolation from the popular standards of society, culture, or family contributes to alienation. When a man is cut off from that which is significant in his family or culture, he assigns a low value to the goals and beliefs that were important to the people around him. He tries to divorce himself from his past, but the separation is more intellectual than social. As a result, the lonely person is not found isolated on an island by himself but is found huddled in the midst of a crowd feeling lost. John Donne said it centuries ago, but it is still true:

> No man is an island of itself; every man is a piece of a continent, a part of the main. If a clod be washed away by the sea, Europe is the less. . . . Any man's death diminishes me, because I am involved in mankind; and therefore never send to know for whom the bell tolls; it tolls for thee![4]

5. *Self-estrangement*. Erich Fromm suggests that this dimension of alienation leads to experiencing one's self as

alien in his own body.[5] It leads to living in terms of what other people think, a blind conformity to the expectations of other people without any intrinsic meaning. This behavior leaves a hollow feeling that does not go away no matter what form of withdrawal a man chooses: drugs, alcohol, sex. Why? He cannot get away from himself.

As a teenager turning adult, Max was fast alienating himself from the people around him. His school counselor had asked me to see if I could find ways to motivate him to complete his education and move on to more exciting things in life. He was failing most of his courses for the semester. Instead of going to class regularly and handing in his homework on time, the boy sat in his room staring at the cracks in the floor and letting his mind spin into oblivion.

His parents loved him dearly, but the depth of their affection had never penetrated his troubled mind. Although he had been born in the United States, he had spent most of his years overseas shifting from post to post. Abroad he tried to be American. In America he acted out cultural habits he had learned to enjoy overseas.

In this complexity of contradictory demands Max had isolated himself from cultural norms and was seriously questioning the religious values of his parents. He felt powerless to break out of the isolation into which he had spun himself. At this point in his adolescence, life had no meaning. He felt estranged, and he was continually being rejected at school. He was considered socially inept and was generally bypassed by both peers and teachers, who took little interest in invading his loneliness.

My task was to try to help Max discover the creativeness buried deep inside him—his mechanical genius and his empathetic concern for disadvantaged people in underdeveloped nations that he had visited. Since his parents were on another overseas tour, the boy had a lot of time on his hands, especially on weekends and holidays. Together we began to explore how solitude can be turned into productiveness rather than be spent groveling in the misery of aloneness.

Creative Loneliness

The answer to man's loneliness lies in creative affirmation of life and the determination to find being alone an exciting, positive experience rather than a negative one. One caution is important here: to renounce your individuality and become submerged in dependence on someone else or some group of other people is psychological suicide. Moustakas says that man must "accept loneliness, face it, live with it, let it be!"[6] To this Rollo May adds, "Maturity and eventual overcoming of loneliness are possible only as one courageously accepts his aloneness to begin with."[7] God's promise to Joshua becomes available to contemporary man: "I will never leave thee nor forsake thee" (Joshua 1:5; Hebrews 13:5).

No man is immune to loneliness. It hits men and women of all ages in all kinds of circumstances, but it is seldom fatal. It is unpleasant to unbearable, perhaps, but loneliness is not fatal unless a man acts against himself and commits emotional or physical suicide.

Leaders will of necessity experience loneliness. That is the price of moving ahead of the group. Richard Wolff in his book *The Meaning of Loneliness* suggests:

In one sense man must remain alone. He must affirm his uniqueness, not with a sense of pride and haughtiness, but as an individual, as a genuine person. This too is self-inflicted, but necessary in order to establish identity and meaning. Too many lives are empty, devoid of purposes, lived in vexation and vanity. The philosopher-king concluded: "So I hated life, because what is done under the sun was grievous to men, for all is vanity and striving after wind." When life is aimless [and] pointless, absurdity and a feeling of alienation prevail. A great effort is required to overcome nihilism, to affirm life, to discover values, to find values, to find meaning and to be a person—alone under God.[8]

So what is creative loneliness? It is recognizing how valuable you really are to God, accepting yourself as He sees you, and then relating positively to other people. That is why Jesus told the scribe in Mark 12:31 to "love your neighbor as yourself." If you don't like yourself, it will be impossible to believe that other people can like you. So avoid self-imposed loneliness by being involved with other people. And avoid social isolation by refusing to allow too few links to be established with others.

Man was created a relational being and finds his identity with the universe in relationships with God and his neighbors. Pick for your relationships those who love you, accept you, and will allow you to be yourself without tryng to force you into their preconceived mold of what you ought to become. And remember: your desire to receive must be matched by your desire to give (Acts 20:35).

Relationships among members of both sexes are important throughout life. It is true that when a man marries he is to retain an emotional and sexual fidelity to his mate. But this does not preclude having friends of both sexes who are just that—friends. The secret of maturing relationships in escaping the clutches of loneliness is learning how to let friendships develop into fellowship without becoming compulsive, possessive, or sexual.

Let your alone times be times of creative excitement. After all, John Milton wrote *Paradise Lost* while he was blind and alone. John Wycliffe translated the Bible into English while he was alone and in prison. John Bunyan wrote *Pilgrim's Progress* alone in jail. Some of Paul's most important epistles were written from the solitude of a prison cell. Solitude does not require a feeling of loneliness. Rather, being alone allows a man to develop his creativity.

ACHIEVING SELF-ESTEEM

Developing meaningful relationships requires a man to release himself from mere survival in life to contribute constructively to the welfare of other people. The process is developmental and leads to satisfying relationships.

Anticedents of Self-Esteem

In his hierarchy of needs, Abraham Maslow has suggested that there are four tasks to be completed before a person can release his creative energies and contribute constructively to his generation.[9] He calls these "D" motives (for "doing") because a man must work to complete these basic tasks.

1. *Physical.* The first task of a man is knowing who he is and moving toward the development of meaningful relationships to handle his physical needs. These are primarily biological and have to do with the basic needs for oxygen, liquid, food, control of elimination processes, pain, heat and cold. These are basic physiological needs that must be satisfied or else man dies.

Closely related to the physiological needs, although not essential for survival, is the sex drive. Studies indicate that a male or a female can live an entire lifetime without one sexual orgasm and not suffer emotionally or physiologically from the deprivation. But the urgency for sexual fulfillment is so strong it is usually considered as a physical drive. Therefore a man must get a handle on his sexuality as a prerequisite to discovering the true meaning of self-esteem.

The single male must learn to be a sexual person without being driven to sexual performance. For sexuality is something you *are,* not something you do. The married male must learn to channel his sexual energies into communicating love in the marital relationship, and he must be faithful to his wife.

2. *Safety.* The safety need is closely related to the physical need in that it pertains to having food and shelter and know-

ing that there is a place where a person can be shut in safely from outside attacks. A child in growing up must know that he is safe in his family home, a place to retreat from the threats of a cruel world.

3. *Love and belongingness.* This is a dual need: the need to be loved at home and still be free to belong to a peer culture. If a man has not been able to make this adjustment in his adolescent years he may well have difficulty in feeling loved in a nonsexual relationship and be driven to promiscuity. To be safe at home and surrounded by love is wonderful. But it must be balanced by the freedom to relate to friends outside the home in the contemporary world. When these two dimensions are balanced, a young person feels loved and knows he belongs.

Self-esteem. This is the highest of the "D" motives and is the point at which a person can develop his uniqueness—his gifts and talents—to make a contribution to his generation. Self-esteem is possible when the energies of life are not absorbed in handling the lower needs of physical, safety, or love and belongingness. The youth can then turn his gaze outward rather than inward.

Maurice Wagner suggests that there are three dimensions to self-esteem:

> *Belongingness* is an awareness of being wanted and accepted, of being cared for and enjoyed.
>
> *Worthiness* is a feeling of "I am good" or "I count" or "I am right."
>
> *Competence* is a feeling of adequacy, of courage, of hopefulness, of strength enough to carry out the tasks of daily life-situations.[10]

On the love and belongingness level of the Maslow hierarchy the young man blends into the background and finds that he is safe, secure, accepted, and loved. On the self-esteem level he moves out from the crowd to stand head and shoulders above his peers to make his unique contribution to his generation. He is doing this in order to establish his identity, but it is a positive and a worthwhile goal. In fact, it is essential for emotional maturity.

BECOMING AN ADEQUATE MAN

Developing the kind of relationships that make for effective Christian living requires a man to come to grips with who he is and to offer himself relationally to others. There are at least six steps in the process.

Accept Yourself

Before you can hope to develop positive relationships with other people, both male and female, you must come to grips with yourself. This involves accepting yourself. Take a look in the mirror. Do you like what you see? If you do, be thankful for your physical endowments. If not, is there anything you can do about it? At this point you must learn to distinguish between the changeable and the unchangeable. That which you cannot change you must accept. There are some physical things that cannot be changed. You must learn to live with them.

On the other hand, are there things about yourself that you could change if you wanted to? The real question is: is it worth it? If you don't like something about yourself and want to change it, now is the time to start. Otherwise, accept yourself and don't let it be an impediment to your healthy self-concept. If you want to broaden your shoulders or tighten your abdominal muscles, get involved in bodybuilding. But *do* it—don't just talk about it. Then you can take a quiet pleasure in being yourself and you can find emotional security in being who you are.

Extend Yourself

It is important to reach out and touch someone. Gordon Allport, one of the great Christians in psychology, observed that unless a person develops strong interests outside himself, and yet still remains true to himself, he lives closer to the animal level than to the human level of existence. Maturity, he believes, advances in proportion to the way our lives are decentered from the immediacy of having to cater to bodily needs and our own ego-centeredness.[11]

It is a well-known fact that emotional illness has its roots in self-centeredness. The admonition to reach beyond that limitation of self and be interested in other people is vital to developing healthy relationships. It is a vital part of a strategy for growing beyond narcissistic loneliness.

Relate Warmly to Other People

In reaching out to be involved in the lives of other people it is essential to develop a genuine warmth in relating to them. This involves the full experiencing of an affectional relationship that does not have any erotic overtones. Learning to have an intimate relationship with other people without basing it on romantic or erotic involvements is the beginning of true friendship.

Be Open to New Experiences

Being able to experience all the sensations of being human, the actual sensory and visceral reactions of the body, without having to pinpoint their source is a delightful experience. It involves getting accustomed to new sounds, tastes, fragrances, and other sensations.

In singleness this allows the full experiencing of what it means to be human and spiritual at the same time. In marriage it involves motivation for giving rather than receiving in lovemaking and approximates what William James called a "peak experience" and what Abraham Maslow calls "raptness." It is most intense in the mutual orgasmic response between a Christian husband and wife who are expressing their love in a nonverbal language that words can never convey.

Be Objective About Yourself

Objectivity has two dimensions: insight and humor.

1. *Insight.* Insight means a good understanding of yourself from three perspectives: the way you see yourself, the way others see you, and the way God sees you. It is something like focusing a camera. When you look into the viewer you see two images. As you adjust the lens the images merge and you know the camera is ready to use. Picture three images that need to be brought into alignment: your view, the view of other people, and God's view. When these images synchronize, you are authentic and ready for creative living.

2. *Humor.* Humor represents the ability to laugh when you are sad, to see light in the dark, to know that behind the dark cloud is a silver lining. Humor gives joy in living. A sense of the ridiculous adds flavor to life. Man is so constructed that it is impossible for him to burn a peptic ulcer while he is laughing. So if you have been hitting the antacids lately, maybe you need to take a look at your sense of humor.

My father was a shoe cobbler for 50 years. As I grew up, he taught me his trade and I spent many hours working by his side in the shoe shop. He was a man of few words, having little to say. When I was getting into middle teens and was so intense about life, he bought a sign to put by my jack in the shop. The message was simple: "Don't take life too seriously. You'll never get out of it alive anyhow."

I'll admit I didn't get the message of the sign until many years later. But now that I look back at it, I realize that my father was trying to tell me that I was too intense, too serious. I was so involved in trying to get into the mainstream of life that I was endangering my health and didn't even know it. In fact, it was not until after a couple of serious illnesses that the message of the old sign really filtered through to me. When I stopped taking life so seriously my health improved. I also discovered the difference in doing God's work my way and becoming a channel through which He could accomplish His work.

Be Reality-Oriented

Reality-orientation requires a man to be in close touch with the real world, not the world of fantasy or make-believe. This involves developing the ability to love and create. To do that, man must emerge from childish ties to the family and nature and take responsibility for his own behavior. He must grasp the reality inside and outside himself by developing objectivity and reason. He must see that the aim of life is to live it intensely, to be fully born, to be awake.

There are basically two requisites for the maturity of reality orientation:

1. *Delay of gratification.* To be ready for mature relationships, a man must be able to delay gratifying his wants. He must be able to work now and save for some future purchase or to begin now preparing for tasks that will be evaluated or tested at some future time. He must be so much in charge of who he is that no part of his anatomy can take precedence over his head in decision-making. He must have such a handle on his sexuality that it never rules his will and involves him in promiscuous sexual behavior; he awaits the time he can enjoy full sexual pleasure within the bonds of marriage.

2. *Responsibility for his own behavior.* As long as a man is making excuses, blaming others, or rationalizing away his own behavior, he is living on an immature level. But when he can take responsibility—credit or blame, as the case may be—for his own behavior, he is moving toward a level of maturity that is worthy of adult relationships.

It was interesting to watch our son grow up with two older sisters at home. Whenever anything went wrong in the house and my wife would ask, "Who did it?" Robert would quickly answer, "Sissy do." It had to be either Cindy or Joan, not him. One day in the summer of his sixteenth year, my wife came in from the bedroom end of the house and named something that was out of place. When she asked, "Who did it?" Robert spoke up without hesitation and said, "I did.

Why?" Nita was so startled by our son's sudden admission that she left the room speechless. I had the first glimmer of hope that he was reaching toward adult maturity!

MOVING TOWARD INTIMACY

Erik Erikson in his "Eight Ages of Man" has given an outline of tasks that every adult must go through in order to develop adequate relationships.[12] The task of young adults, Erikson says, is finding intimacy. Intimacy involves the capacity to commit yourself to other people selflessly. For the single male this means to have meaningful adult relationships that are not erotic or sexual but bring out the highest qualities of masculinity or femininity in those people with whom he associates. Failure to make the adjustments that lead to intimacy results in isolation, the avoidance of life's opportunities. This may well result in character problems. Promiscuous sexual behavior is an indication that a person, male or female, is avoiding emotional intimacy and instead is assuming that sexual performance or physical closeness is all there is to intimacy.

Being able to handle adult intimacy is based on successfully completing the tasks of earlier years: developing trust rather than mistrust, autonomy rather than shame and doubt, initiative rather than guilt, industry rather than inferiority, and ego identity rather than role confusion.

The secret to developing mature adult relationships lies in handling the tasks of love that overcome loneliness and isolation: becoming a trusting person, finding a sense of freedom in being one's self, and venturing out into being a man who is masculine in the world of reality.

It is not until a man has reached this level of emotional maturity that he is ready to consider the crucial question of whether he will remain single for a while or launch immediately into marriage and family. Until a man knows who he is and likes being who he is, he is not ready to offer himself to another person for a marriage commitment "until death us do part."

Notes

1. David Riesman, *The Lonely Crowd* (New Haven: Yale University Press, 1950).
2. Paul Tournier, *Escape from Loneliness* (Philadelphia: Westminster Press, 1962).
3. Viktor E. Frankl, *Man's Search for Meaning* (New York: Simon and Schuster, 1959, 1962).
4. John Donne, "Devotions upon Emergent Occasions," in James D. Robertson, ed., *Handbook of Preaching Resources from English Literature* (New York: The MacMillian Company, 1962), p. 87.
5. Erich Fromm, *The Sane Society* (New York: Rinehart, 1955).
6. Clark Moustakas, *Loneliness* (Englewood Cliffs, NJ: Prentice-Hall, 1961).
7. Rollo May, *Man's Search for Himself* (New York: New American Library, 1967).
8. Richard Wolff, *The Meaning of Loneliness* (Wheaton: Key Publishers, 1970).
9. Abraham Maslow, *Motivation and Personality* (New York: Harper, 1970).
10. Maurice Wagner, *The Sensation of Being Somebody* (Grand Rapids: Zondervan, 1975), pp. 32-37.
11. Gordon Allport, *Becoming* (New Haven: Yale University Press, 1955).
12. Erik Erikson, "Eight Ages of Man," in *International Journal of Psychiatry,* 1966, pp. 287-97.

Chapter 4
Perfectionism Versus Being an Authentic Man

Who can describe a perfect man? Intelligent? Athletic? Artistic? Sensitive? Spiritual? He is a combination of all of these qualities plus many more. Whatever a man thinks it takes to be a perfect male can drive him to try to approximate that ideal in his head and attempt to live out that fantasy in everyday life. But the task will be self-defeating.

No scene from ancient history portrays the futility of perfectionism more than that of Alexander the Great standing high in the Himalayas weeping because there were not more worlds for him to conquer. Alexander had everything a man could desire. His body was a spectacular specimen of masculine perfection. He married the most beautiful princesses that his conquering hordes could capture. He was the son of Philip of Macedon, the great Greek king, and raised in a palace with Aristotle as a companion and teacher. Yet Alexander the Great died at age 33 from the complications of alcoholism and venereal disease. He conquered the then-known world but never conquered himself nor came to grips with the true meaning of life.

In less dramatic ways many men fall into the trap of Alexander: the compulsion for perfectionism. They set high goals but fall short of them and grovel in their own disappointment. The energy expended in the effort to attain unrealistic goals robs a man of the fulfilling life he could have if he would pause to consider who he is in the cosmic order of the universe and become a man of God. Gene Getz puts it this way: "In Christianity, you see, there is no contradiction between being a *man's man* and being a gentle man."[1]

MAN IS SPECIAL

Just how special is man? Special enough that man is the first thing in the created universe that God made with His own hands. Custom-made by the hands of God! That is the unique privilege of the human male.

Custom-Made

Genesis 1 gives a thumbnail sketch of the sequence of creation. It points out that God spoke the whole universe into existence by separating light from darkness, then created the intricacies of the mineral, vegetable, and animal kingdoms. God brought perfect ecological balance to Planet Earth. Then He created Adam and placed him in the Garden of Eden to dominate animal life and maintain the ecological balance of the new creation.

Man was created in the image of God as both a rational and relational being (Genesis 1:26,27). As a rational being man was empowered to think, solve problems, be creative, evaluate outcomes, and communicate with other people. He was also designed to maintain an open relationship with the triune God—Father, Son, and Holy Spirit—who had said, "Let us make man" (Genesis 1:26-28). Maintaining a constant relationship with the Creator God is a major function of what it means to be a man.

The rest of creation had been brought into being by God's voice penetrating the vacuum of space, but with man it was different. God took the dust of the earth and formed the configuration of the male body, then endowed it with the finest functions of sensory, motor, circulatory, neurological, and hormonal efficiency in His universe (Genesis 2:7). Into this lifeless form God breathed the breath of life, and man became a living soul. The human male body is the first thing God made with His own hands, giving man the distinction of being custom-made by God Himself.

No matter what men may have done to distort God's

original handiwork, man is unique and special. He represents the finest form of God's creative genius. So the next time you look at yourself in the mirror, remember that your body was custom-made by God. You might also want to look at how well you are taking care of your body. After all, it is not really your own; it is the temple of the Holy Spirit (1 Corinthians 6:19,20). Many men do not recognize how special they really are. They abuse their bodies by poor health habits and physical abuse. Determine that you are going to treat your body with the deference that is due to divine creation.

When confronted with the purpose of being, many men ask such questions as, "Why was I born?" or "Why am I here?" God's Word gives us four approaches in answering the age-old questions of human existence.

Four Tasks

There are at least four tasks that man was designed to fulfill in his personal relationship with God.

1. *Love God.* In the Jewish tradition Deuteronomy 6:4,5 is known as the *Shema* or Great Commandment. A Greek version of this commandment appears in the first three Gospels, emphasizing the importance of man's relationship with God. The Commandment tells us that the first obligation of man is to love God. To love God in the way He wants us to love Him involves the total human personality. Moses listed three ways in which man can love God: with his heart, his soul, and his might.

Studies of human behavior have defined three major dimensions of the human personality and have devised a detailed outline to explain each function. These are called the cognitive domain, the affective domain, and the psychomotor domain.

The cognitive domain has to do with thinking. It relates to intelligence and incorporates both knowledge and wisdom. The processes of thinking and learning as well as the application of learning through wisdom in everyday life are what *heart* means in the Old Testament.

In the New Testament two words are used to convey this idea from the Old Testament. (Greek was the language used by Jesus and the Gospel writers.) Early Greek philosophers felt that the concept "heart" was too broad, so they coined the word "mind" to explain part of the thinking process. "Wisdom" is the word they used to express the application of knowledge; they retained the word "heart" to refer to the learning process of gaining knowledge. So when speaking of loving God as Moses had written, Jesus used both "heart" and "mind" in order to be clearly understood by the Greek-speaking crowds of His day (Mark 12:28-30). Paul used the same dichotomy in Philippians 4:6,7 when he talked about the peace that comes from trusting prayer. Simply, then, the Old Testament used "heart" to refer to both knowledge and wisdom, but in the New Testament "heart" is limited more to knowledge and "mind" is used to convey the application of knowledge in the form of wisdom. Using a computer model, heart is the "input" and mind the "output" of the human thinking process.

To love God in the way He wants to be loved requires us to study His Word, to hide its precepts in our heart, and to apply its principles to everyday living. David could say, "Thy word have I hid in mine heart, that I might not sin against thee" and "Thy word is a lamp unto my feet and a light unto my path" (Psalm 119:11,105).

As noted in an earlier chapter, love is an attitude. It begins as a thought in the mind. We use the word "stance" to describe a physical attitude or postural direction. Picture Mark Spitz as he stands poised on the edge of the Olympic pool ready to slice into the water and win another gold medal. Visualize Jimmy Conner poised to send a volley across the net to Bjorn Borg or Pete Rose arched to hit another home run or Dr. J. stretching to sink another basket. As each athlete takes a differing stance to respond, the man of God develops mental attitudes that will help him respond efficiently to the opportunities of life.

To love God with the heart means that we study His Word and prepare ourselves to respond consistently to the opportunities of life in ways that demonstrate to Him and to others that our motivation is rooted in God's Word and our perception of His will for us.

"Soul" is used in the Old Testament to describe emotions. This includes motivation and excitement. To love with the soul is to enjoy service for God and get a gentle pleasure out of responding to our perception of His will for our lives. David says in Psalm 25:1, "Unto thee, O Lord, do I lift up my soul" and in Psalm 40:8, "I delight to do thy will, O my God: yea, thy law is within my heart."

This feeling of excitement that comes from doing God's will lies in what psychologists called the affective domain, the area of emotionality and feeling. It is in loving God with the soul that the joy of salvation is experienced. This interaction of a shared love with the divine brings man into an intimate relationship with God that transcends any human form of relationship.

To love God with the *might* requires man to put into behavioral demonstration the knowledge he has and the love he feels for God. There is no way an attitude can be measured. Like intelligence, an attitude can only be inferred by behavioral demonstration. Jesus uses the term "strength" to express this concept in Mark 12:29.

I could say to my wife, "I love you. Bring me a cup of tea." Her response would be, "I love you too. Go get it yourself." You see, she and I both know that love does not make demands. If I really want to say "I love you" to my wife and I want a cup of tea, I know to choose Monday night. I prepare two cups of tea with ¼ grain of saccharin and 3 drops of lemon juice, then I take it into the family room and put it on the coffee table between the divan and TV. After 32 years of marriage I know there is nothing my wife enjoys more than Monday night football. So I prepare the tea while she gets all settled to referee the game from divan-side. (This is one of the pleasures she learned from her father that I have made no attempt to change.)

To love God in the way He wants to be loved requires a man to seek to know more about God and His Word and to apply its precepts in everyday life through wise choices and behavior. Man was designed to enjoy the full spectrum of excitement that accompanies living in harmony with God's Word and to become deliberately involved in those kinds of things that bring fulfillment to himself and honor to God.

2. *Fear God.* Solomon, in Ecclesiastes 12:13, says that it is the duty of man to fear God. This fear involves reverence, respect, and awe for the privilege of a personal relationship with God. David declares, "The fear of the Lord is the beginning of wisdom: a good understanding have all they that do his commandments; his praise endureth forever" (Psalm 111:10).

As a father never holds his children off in sheer panic, so a loving God does not keep His children at bay. In fact, we are encouraged to call Him "Father" (Romans 8:15) and to come boldly into His presence (Hebrews 4:16). God is pictured by Jesus as One who delights in giving good things to His children (Matthew 7:7-11).

One of the distinctions of a man of God is that he has a healthy respect for God. Man does not cower from God's presence, but seeks ways to honor Him and emulate the principles of Biblical living in everyday life. Rather than being a sign of weakness, the fear of the Lord opens the way for the wisdom of God, through the enlightenment of the Holy Spirit, to be applied in everyday personal and business affairs.

Gene was a successful contractor. He bid on a set of municipal buildings to be constructed in a Midwestern city. His was the lowest bid, and it would have yielded a fair profit. He was told, however, that before his bid could be accepted by the commissioners that there would have to be a "kickback" under the table. Gene, being a consistent Christian, an elder in his church, and a Sunday school teacher, refused. The contract was granted to a rival firm.

When Gene shared this information with me he was not bitter—only perplexed. We both knew he had done the right thing. To the surprise of both of us, a large farm on the edge of a neighboring town went on the market unexpectedly and was available at an unbelievably low price. Gene bought it and started subdividing the sections. When he completed the project, Gene told me that he had made twice as much from the subdivision as he would have made from the municipal contract. This is not a promise that every sacrifice for the cause of Christ is going to have monetary gain, but it does indicate that a perceived loss in one area of life may find compensation through wisdom for success in another project.

3. *Obey God.* Obedience to God is closely related to reverence for God. In fact, the commands are found in the same verse (Ecclesiastes 12:13). Both the Old and New Testament are replete with commands to obey God, serve Him, and carry out His commandments consistently. This is the secret of discipleship. God does not always give reasons for His expectations, but He does promise that faithful adherence to them will have a positive result now and in eternity.

The "thou shalts" of Scripture are just as important as the "thou shalt nots." Too much of the time we get so tied up with lists of what to do that we overlook other commandments that go undone. Sins of omission are just as devastating to both human and divine relationships as are the sins of commission. The dialogue between Jesus and the rich young ruler makes this crystal clear. Enumeration of sins not to commit in the Ten Commandments (Exodus 20:1-17) are balanced by the commandments to witness and love (Matthew 28:19,20; John 15:12).

4. *Worship God.* Not only does God want us to love Him,

to have a healthy reverence for who He is, and to obey Him, but He also desires for us to worship Him. One of the final pictures of the New Testament is taken from a vision of the Apostle John on the Isle of Patmos. There he saw a preview of what is currently transpiring in heaven and what the future holds. Revelation 4:11 shows the hosts of heaven engaged in constant worship of the Christ: "Thou art worthy, O Lord, to receive glory and honor and power: for thou hast created all things, and for thy pleasure they are and were created."

David suggests that God lives in or inhabits the praises of men who worship Him, and that He is enthroned by these praises (Psalm 22:3). God lives with a man who loves respects, and obeys Him. And a life of love, reverence, and obedience becomes a continuing act of worship.

ORDERED PRIORITIES

Perfectionism is put into perspective when a man orders the priorities of his life according to Biblical principles.

Priority One: Love God

The elaboration of Jesus in the *Shema* helps us set the order correctly. Mark puts it this way: "And thou shalt love the Lord thy God with all thy heart, and with all thy soul, and with all thy mind, and with all thy strength: this is the first commandment. And the second is like, namely this, Thou shalt love thy neighbor as thyself. There is none other commandment greater than these (Mark 12:30,31). Matthew leaves out strength: "Thou shalt love the Lord thy God with all thy heart, and with all thy soul, and with all thy mind. This is the first and great commandment. And the second is like unto it, Thou shalt love thy neighbor as thyself. On these two commandments hang all the law and the prophets" (Matthew 22:37-40). And Luke records: "Thou shalt love the Lord thy God with all thy heart, and with all thy soul, and with all thy strength, and with all thy mind; and thy neighbor as thyself" (Luke 10:27).

Moses and the first three Gospel writers agree that the great Commandment requires a man to love God with the entire human personality. They all agree that this love begins on a cognitive level of loving with the heart. Matthew and Mark elaborate on the Hebrew by using heart and mind to cover the cognitive aspect of a love relationship with God. All three writers agree that there is an affective or feeling dimension in loving God with all the soul and allow for emotionality to be a vital part of man's love life. What Moses called "might" in the Hebrew both Mark and Luke call "strength" from the Greek perspective. Both concepts imply action and energy, overt behavior that demonstrates the internal qualities of love.

Priority Two: Love Yourself

To emphasize that a man must have love for himself as a prerequisite to loving his neighbor may seem strange to men whose teaching has been "other"-oriented. When I was growing up in a conservative Christian home the formula was J-O-Y: Jesus, others, yourself. However, this is not what Jesus says, according to Mark. Jesus said that a man is to love his neighbor, but *as* he loves himself.

The man who does not love himself will not have the capacity to love others, whether they are of the immediate family or those of the neighborhood. Love must be a reciprocal relationship: God loves man, man loves God. This basic concept frees a man from the compulsion for perfectionism in performance for himself or others and sets him free to become actualized in Christ.

When the loving nature of a man is rooted in a personal relationship with God, he will draw on divine strength to become a loving person in human relationships. The mutuality of this giving and sharing and accepting love eliminates the selfishness and narcissism that Freud warned against and that fragment so many human relationships.

The man who knows he is loved by God is free to share

love with other people. But this love must be filtered through a self-concept that is rooted in a love for God. In Chapter 3 we discussed the steps necessary to achieve the kind of self-esteem that comes from an intimate relationship with the Father through Jesus Christ and the witness of the Holy Spirit.

1. Accept yourself
2. Extend yourself
3. Relate warmly to other people
4. Be open to new experiences
5. Be objective about yourself
6. Be reality-oriented.

This acceptance of self because of total acceptance by God makes it possible for a man to reach out to his neighbors and love each one adequately.

Priority Three: Love Your Neighbor

Luke tells us that the lawyer who asked Jesus about the Great Commandment was trying to tempt Him. Apparently pricked by the truth of the answer that Jesus gave from Deuteronomy 6:4,5, the lawyer tried to justify himself by asking Jesus to define what he meant by "neighbor." Then follows the story of the Good Samaritan.

In family living it is appropriate to see the family relationship as an expanding set of concentric circles. For the married man, his closest neighbor should be his wife, followed by their children, the extended family, and then career, church, and civic responsibilities. For the single man the circle begins with family, both immediate and extended, and then into community relationships of social, vocational, spiritual, and civic nature.

The order in which a man establishes the priorities of his life tells much about him spiritually and emotionally. When the divine order is followed, healthfulness in relationships results. When the priorities are disordered, fragmentation and emotional stress are inevitable. The man who is more involved with his career than his wife, family, and personal spiritual development is headed for problems.

To all observers, Jack was a success. He had graduated from college with honors, had secured a position with a prestigious firm, and was rapidly climbing the ladder of success into top management. It was not until his wife had an affair with his best friend that Jack realized that his devotion to his career was selfishness of a gross degree and that his neglect of his wife and her needs was as much a sin as her affair. Through counseling and prayer he reordered his priorities and the marriage has been restored.

Fred was the spiritual head of his household. In fact, he was so busy with church activities that he really didn't leave much time for his wife and children. Every night of the week was occupied in some church activity: Sunday school and church on Sunday morning, with church again on Sunday night, with possibly a church board meeting or a leadership conference during the afternoon. Monday night was Sunday school visitation, Tuesday night nursing home ministry, Wednesday night church, Thursday night special activities with the boys of the church, either athletic or instructional. Friday night he hosted a Bible study and prayer group in his home, and Saturday night was when the men's fellowship met.

It was at the end of a retreat for married couples that Fred's wife was able to communicate to him her loneliness and how much she needed his help with the children. Fred, his wife, and I sat down and redistributed his time so he could have time for the family. The result was spectacular. Other people in the church were eager to take over the responsibilities that Fred became willing to delegate. The work of the Lord didn't suffer. In fact, it flourished because more individuals became involved in the Christian service Fred relinquished. Fred's family developed a togetherness they had never experienced before.

THE AUTHENTIC MAN

In Chapter 3 the process of achieving self-esteem was introduced, and it concluded with a discussion of how to become an adequate male. It was noted that the first four levels of Maslow's need hierarchy are "D" motives, things that have to be worked through and resolved in order to be emotionally healthy. These included physical needs, safety needs, love and belongingness needs, and the need for self-esteem.

The next set of needs in the hierarchy represents what Maslow called "B" motives, for "being." If Maslow is right—and much research supports his hypothesis—a person shifts gears in moving from the "D" motives to the "B" motives. A man stops working, slips into overdrive, and flows as the spontaneous personality he has become as a result of resolving his lower needs. The people who achieve this level of maturity Maslow called "self-actualizers." He illustrated the concept by such examples as Abraham Lincoln, Walt Whitman, Albert Schweitzer, Eleanor Roosevelt, and others whose life was devoted to a cause in behalf of their fellowmen rather than for their own personal aggrandizement.

The interesting thing about the self-actualizer is that he never knows he is one. The minute a man adopts the label of "self-actualizer" he indicates that he is operating on a lower level: self-esteem, love and belongingness, or even safety. The true actualizer is so completely free from self-centered behavior that he is giving and being and not aware that his behavior is being perceived as actualizing. Studies indicate that actualizers get more out of life and enjoy it more than most other people.

Some Christians have difficulty with the concept of *self-*actualization, suggesting that it by definition represents behavior that is self-centered. To overcome this semantic drawback from what appears to be a healthy Biblical concept

I have coined the word *Christ-actualization*. I believe this is the meaning of Galatians 2:20, where Paul says, "I am crucified with Christ: nevertheless I live; yet not I, but Christ liveth in me; and the life which I now live in the flesh I live by the faith of the Son of God, who loved me and gave himself for me."

Paul had become so identified with the claims of Christ that the free flow of his personality was that of reflecting the presence of the indwelling Christ. Yet his was not a haughty attitude, for he said:

> Brethren, I count not myself to have apprehended, but this one thing I do: forgetting those things which are behind and reaching forth unto those things which are before, I press toward the mark for the prize of the high calling of God in Christ Jesus (Philippians 3:13,14).

Paul's striving was not to fulfill a personal need; it was to explore more of the dimensions of the kingdom of God and the will of God for his life. It involved a spiritual maturity in both depth and breadth, a process that continues for every man as long as he lives.

In *Healing Love,* Shostrom and Montgomery point out that following Biblical principles makes it possible for the Christian man to become an actualizing personality more readily than many other contemporary lifestyles. My own research, including a personal discussion with Everett Shostrom, the leading interpreter of Maslow today, has led me to conclude that the Christian has an advantage in the actualizing process. By using the Scriptures as principles for living and the guidance of the Holy Spirit for insight, the Christian can rise to the point of self-actualization much as cream rises to the top of a can of fresh milk. And, through Christ, he goes a step further. As a result, I have adjusted the usual portrayal of the hierarchy of human needs presented by Maslow and his interpreters by adding another level to the top of the pyramid:

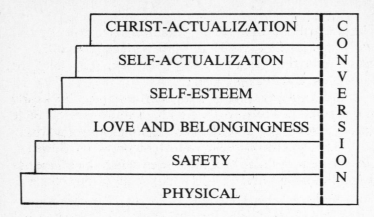

As I have continued to study the processes of actualization, I have become more and more convinced that a Christian man can go beyond the world's concept of adequacy or authenticity to actualize in Christ and fulfill the will of God in this life while preparing for the life to come. For the man who comes to Christ late in life and has not had a lifetime to resolve the needs represented by the "D" motives, I believe that consistent study of the Bible coupled with a desire to be led by the Holy Spirit can streamline the process. This is why I believe that many new Christians put some long-standing Christians to shame when it comes to their dedication to Christ and commitment to Christian service. They are allowing their new personal relationships with Christ to help them resolve the problems they had not faced adequately before their conversion.

But, young or old, Christ-actualization is a process. "The testimony of the actualizing Christian," Shostrom and Montgomery conclude, "is not that he or she is perfect, but rather that he or she is *being perfected* by the healing love and power of God. The process of being made whole involves gradual transformation of one's entire being."[2]

No, man does not need to seek his perfection in things of this world or even to attempt to prove who or what he is. He needs to find his authenticity as a person in becoming a

Christ-actualized personality. Admittedly, it is the kind of search that is easier to achieve when begun in youth, but no man is too old to begin the quest to be completely identified with Christ and His kingdom.

It was nearing the end of a long day in Africa. Since early morning Ted had been working with his students at the Bible training center. Teaching classes all morning and supervising work activities and counseling all afternoon were followed in the evening with the showing of a science film to give the national pastors-in-training insight into some of the mysteries unveiled by scientific research.

It was past nine as Ted put away the projector and prepared to retire to the mission house. Tabo, one of the more promising students, came over to the missionary. Running his hands up and down the white man's arms, he said, "You feel human, but the way you love us sometimes we think you are divine."

There are times when the actualizer appears to be from another world, but he very much has his feet grounded on solid earth. It is just that he marches to the beat of a different drum because he is "being" rather than "doing," and the free flow of his personality takes on an aura that makes him appear to be very different from his fellowmen.

Notes

1. Gene Getz, *The Measure of a Man* (Glendale: Regal Books, 1974), p. 136.
2. Everett L. Shostrom and Dan Montgomery, *Healing Love* (Nashville: Abingdon, 1978), p. 83.

Ed.—The dotted line in the diagram is used to indicate that Christian conversion can speed the process of actualization.

Chapter 5
Competition Versus Living Out God's Forgiveness

Although there are differences from culture to culture, competition seems to be an inevitable part of the human condition. Called "aggression" by students of human behavior and "survival of the fittest" by students of animal behavior, competition appears to be a universal drive. How and when this competition shows itself is culturally learned, and the degree to which it is accepted is part of the moral as well as the legal codes of the culture.

COMPETITION OUT OF CONTROL

When I was living in Africa I learned that an ancient code of the jungle in one of the sub-Sahara regions differentiated between murder and mercy-killing in this way. If you were going to kill a man, you had to make sure your machete was sharp enough to sever his head from his body with one blow. If you were able to sever the head from the shoulders in one swift blow, it was considered merciful and you had sent the victim into the next phase of reincarnation. You had done the victim a favor and would not be punished. On the other hand, if the machete were dull and it took two blows to make the severing complete, it would hurt the individual. You would be judged by the laws of the jungle for murder because of a serious violation of human rights.

Fortunately, this custom has long since ceased to exist, but the motivation behind it can be found in societies around the world. It is called "good business" or "Sorry, but that's the way the cookie crumbles." Whatever methods are necessary to win in physical, emotional, social, political, or financial struggles are acceptable. Of course this is completely opposite to what the Bible teaches about the kingdom of heaven. In God's economy it is the poor in spirit who possess the kingdom and it is the meek who inherit the earth (Matthew 5:3,5).

We noted in the previous chapter that man was custom-made by the hand of God. At that time he was given two assignments in life. Adam was instructed to "Be fruitful and multiply, and replenish the earth, and subdue it; and have dominion over the fish of the sea and over the fowl of the air and over every living thing that moveth upon the earth." (Genesis 1:28). Notice two commandments: 1) reproduce and fill up the earth with children, and 2) dominate the created world by maintaining the ecological balance of the biosphere we now call Planet Earth.

On both scores man has failed miserably. Overpopulation has brought the earth to the point of self-destruction, so that hunger and malnutrition are a way of life—closer to death than life—in many parts of the world. Misuse of the environment—animal and mineral—has led to the extinction of species of animals, fish, and fowl that subsequent generations will never have the pleasure of admiring. Abuses of the environment, both terrestrial and atmospheric, have brought about the energy crunch and threaten to blight land, sea, and air.

Such failure of man to fulfill his created purposes is in a large part due to inordinate competition: competition for mates, lands, possessions, and political control of weaker peoples. How far this is from God's plan for the earth and the people He has placed on it! Only the promises of the book of Revelation related to the millennial reign of Christ give hope that competition and vicious aggressiveness will ultimately prove to be futile and that there will really come a time when mankind "shall beat their swords into plowshares, and their spears into pruninghooks; nation shall not lift up sword against nation, neither shall they learn war anymore" (Isaiah 2:4). Increased competition will be a signal of Christ's return, He says in Matthew 24:3-14.

COMPETITION UNDER CONTROL

On a personal level, every man must develop adequacy. This includes his headship in the family (Ephesians 5:23) and the degree of assertiveness necessary to perform adequately on his job. Assertiveness without aggression is the balance that allows a man to be masculine without being driven by the compulsive behavior that will ruin him emotionally and destroy meaningful relationships with other people. Erik Erikson describes this kind of healthy productive activity and calls it *generativity*. It is a major goal of life and lies developmentally in the seventh of Erikson's "Eight Ages of Man."[1]

Generativity is not something that is discovered suddenly in adulthood; it is the product of a lifelong quest for excellence as a person. It is rooted in the self-concept of the male child and grows through various stages of psychosocial development.

The six steps leading to adult male generativity are developmental in nature. Each early crisis must be handled adequately before the person is free to move on to a higher level of development. If this does not happen at the age desired, Erikson suggested, the older male will have become fixated at the earlier level. He must go back and develop the tasks necessary to be free to move on to the next higher level of functioning if he is to experience generativity and integrity.

Trust

The challenge of the first year of life is to become a trusting person. During this time the child is totally dependent on other people to care for his love and survival needs. He needs both mother and father to cuddle and nurture him, to tend to his needs, and to play with him. Infant boys who are cared for affectionately and have their needs adequately met learn to trust their environment and those who are in it. Forming trust begins with the mother, is fostered by the father, and is carried on by siblings and members of the extended family. If not, the child tends to become fearful and mistrusting—mistrusting himself as well as others.

Autonomy

The second task of the growing male is to become an autonomous individual. This crisis lies in the second and third years of life. He needs time and space to learn to walk, talk, and act independently of constant adult supervision. The child who is allowed the necessary amount of freedom at this point learns to deal more adequately with later situations. If autonomy is stymied through inconsistent discipline, over-protectiveness, or disapproval at attempts toward autonomy, the child will develop a tendency toward shame and doubt. Such negative emotions will interfere with creativity early in life and will plant the seeds for compulsive behavior to meet the expectations of others and to overcompensate for perceived weaknesses or failures.

Initiative

Between ages four and five, the last of the preschool years, the child needs opportunities to express his initiative. If he does not have this freedom, guilt will be the result. He can come to the place that he feels guilty for the most insignificant inadequacies or failures. The child whose activities, questions, and general creative play are encouraged by parents and siblings finds it easier to become assertive as an adult, to make good decisions and to be more adventurous. If he is placed under too many restrictions at this tender age he will develop feelings of guilt when trying to be expressive. He will hesitate to move out on his own or to make decisions and follow through with them.

Industry

The opportunity of the elementary school years is that of industry. Erikson explains it this way:

While all children at times need to be left alone in solitary play or in later years in the company of books and radio, motion pictures and television, and while all children need their hours and days of make-believe in games, they all, sooner or later, become dissatisfied and disgruntled without a sense of being able to make things and make them well and even perfectly: it is this that I have called the *sense of industry*. Without this, even the best-entertained child soon acts exploited. It is as if he knows and his society knows that now that he is psychologically already a rudimentary parent, he must begin to be something of a worker and potential provider before becoming a biological parent. With the on-coming latency period, then, the advancing child forgets, or rather quietly "sublimates"—that is, applied to concrete pursuits and approved goals—the drives which have made him dream and play. He now learns to win recognition by producing things. He develops perseverence and adjusts himself to the inorganic laws of the tool world and can become an eager and absorbed unit of a productive situation.[2]

The boy who is not free to develop this sense of industry in the elementary school years is almost destined to develop the famed "inferiority complex." Alfred Adler coined the term in the early part of the twentieth century to describe a behavior that is self-defeating in life. Inferiority develops when parents and teachers become annoyed with a child's first attempts at self-initiated activities and are too severe in their criticisms of his work or rejecting of his attempts at industriousness. This will encourage him to lose interest in completing future tasks and lead him to the expression "I can't." Actually, there is no such thing as "I can't." It is only "I won't," and in many cases with the addition of "and I dare you to try to make me."

Every creative attempt of a growing child will not be perfect. How the adults in his life handle these attempts at creativity and initiative, however, will set him free to keep trying—and to refine his efficiency—or else destine him to withdraw from opportunities to initiate and create. This is frequently the history of the young man who seeks out women who will dominate him and lead him to marry a mother image who will continue to make decisions for him.

Brad was that kind of man. He dated only older girls who took the lead in social and romantic behavior and, ultimately, in their premarital sexual affairs. It was not until they were in the third year of their marriage that he realized he had surrendered to her the decision-making of their relationship and that she was calling the shots on both their budget and sex life. He came for counseling because he was being smothered by a surrogate mother rather than being captivated by a sensitive lover. He couldn't do anything to suit his wife, not even making love to her satisfaction. He was becoming impotent.

Identity

The task of the adolescent male is to find his identity as a man. This challenge usually lasts from ages 12 to 20. It is at this point that the boy-becoming-man integrates his previous experiences into a sense of ego identity. He determines what he wants out of life, what he believes in, and who he really is. If he is not free to develop this ego identity, the result will be role confusion.

Erickson suggests that this is probably the most important conflict the male faces in his lifetime. If it is not resolved adequately he will experiment with homosexuality, bisexuality, and/or promiscuous heterosexuality. He may fixate on one of these faulty behaviors as a way of life. Since this is also the time when attitudes and values are being crystallized into guidelines for living, it is essential that the adolescent male be given a faith to live by and be exposed to adult male models who exemplify these values.

Studies have indicated that the average age of conversion in evangelical churches is between 12 and 13. Youths who find their ego identity in a personal relationship with Christ by the time they reach age 13 have a much better chance of adopting attitudes and values that will hold them steady during the crisis of the teen years as they live a Christian life. Hebrews 2:18 and 4:14-16 are a reminder to the young male that Jesus experienced all of the temptations of teens but was nevertheless faithful to the principles of the kingdom of God, enumerated in both the Old and New Testaments. It is at this age that the youth is free to explore the gift of singleness Paul talks about in I Corinthians 7 until he makes the choice for marriage. Marriage is elective: it is not a required course in life. Walt Menninger in his book *Happiness Without Sex* has some helpful things to say about the matter.[3]

Intimacy

The young man who has handled ego identity adequately and knows who he is as a single male can have intimate, nonerotic relationships with both men and women. He explores the dimensions of friendships that are neither romantic nor erotic. In fact, until the young man has explored singleness he is not ready for marriage. To expect to find happiness in a person of the complementary sex is an exercise in futility. The intimate person is the one who trusts, shares, and gives of himself emotionally, spiritually, and mentally without need for sexual expression. He can be a nondemanding friend and an intimate listener without having to perform as a physical lover.

Marriage is not a guarantee of intimacy. Some of the most unhappy people are those who married with the expectations of solving their problems, only to find that they are as isolated in marriage as they were before marriage. In fact, Menninger suggests that promiscuous sexual behavior is an evidence of the lack of emotional intimacy. The isolated male feels alone in the crowd, unfulfilled on the job, and unsatisfied in the bed of another person, whether male or female.

Generativity

The adult male who has learned to be trusting, autonomous, spontaneous in initiative, and industrious, and has also discovered his ego identity and is able to maintain intimate relationships with other people, is free to explore the dimensions of generativity. Erikson says that generativity is work productiveness not for himself but for the succeeding generation. "*Generativity,* then, is primarily the concern for establishing and guiding the next generation."[4]

The question is not the expending of energy but the motivation behind this involvement. If a man is working hard and producing for the benefit of his wife and children, he is involved in generativity. If, on the other hand, he is caught up in the quest for ego satisfaction and personal fulfillment—the limelight or the accolades that come from his compulsive workaholic behavior—he is locked into what Erikson calls "self-absorption."

How can a man tell when this is true of him? When he would rather stay on the job than go home and face the normal problems of marriage and family, he is involved in self-absorption. If, on the other hand, he works hard and enjoys his work because he knows he is providing adequately for his wife and family, he is enjoying the fruits of generativity. He will be able to leave the job on the job, shift gears emotionally, and anticipate going home to work and play with his wife and children, no matter what their ages. Generativity brings out vocational excellence in a man but also frees him to relax with his family and be involved in their education, games, fun, and leisure. It frees a man from the competition of the "rat race" for materialism and allows him to move freely in loving, working, and playing.

Freud was once asked what was the most important task in a man's life. He responded, "*Leben und arbeiten*" (loving and working), and he added, "in that order." When a man allows his work to interfere with his love life, he is working too hard! He has become a workaholic, which can be as addictive as any of the other life-controlling problems: alcoholism, drug abuse, or sexual infidelity.

BEYOND COMPETITION

In the previous chapter we noted that there is a place in Christ where a man can cease from the struggles of meeting lower-level needs and become a Christ-actualized personality. The transition involves both surrender and forgiveness.

Surrender

When a man surrenders his life to Christ, he ceases compulsive competition for the things of this world and finds rest in Christ. He ceases from labor in order to survive or succeed. Rather, he engages in a high level of involvement to do those things which are consistent with the will of God.

The process begins when a man comes to grips with his mortality and finiteness: everyone has sinned and fallen short of God's goals, according to Romans 3:23. Paul says to confess verbally that Christ is the Son of God and Lord of your life and believe that He died for your sins and arose from the dead to complete your salvation. You will then become a son of God (Romans 10:9,10; 8:14-17). As new problems arise and you become aware of your inadequacies, or as God reveals to you new dimensions of His will, you maintain your relationship with Him by confessing your sins (I John 1:9). This brings you to the position of enjoying the "rest" of God while actively engaged in productive, creative living:

> There remaineth therefore a rest to the people of God. For he that is entered into his rest, he also hath ceased from his own works, as God did from his. Let us labor therefore to enter into that rest, lest any man fall after the same example of unbelief (Hebrews 4:9-11).

The work productiveness of the Christian man, whether it be on the job or in the home, community, or church, is that labor of love which is void of the tensions of competition and the high levels of anxiety that competitiveness brings.

For some men the process of surrender to God appears to be difficult. Western man has been taught competitiveness for so long that he finds his work habits and attitudes difficult to change. However, the operation of the Holy Spirit in the life of the believing man can make the Word of God come alive and show him ways of responding spiritually to the challenges of life. This in turn brings about a noticeable personality change as the Christian man takes on the character of God and image of Christ in his everyday life.

In order for this to happen, the power of forgiveness must be comprehended and experienced.

Receiving Forgiveness

Forgiveness is the process in which two people who have been at odds no longer dwell on their differences and instead start a new relationship as though nothing negative had occurred.

Blaine was a very troubled man when he called me for an appointment. He had attended one of the couples' retreats I had conducted. During the weekend he didn't have the courage to seek me out for personal consultation. A few weeks later, however, he called for an appointment. That he had to miss a day of work and drive 100 miles each way indicated he was hurting badly.

We were not long into the session when he spilled the sordid story of being unfaithful to his wife in a moment of loneliness and isolation when on a job that had taken him out of town for several days. He said he had confessed the adultery to his wife and that she had been accepting and forgiving. He had shared the sin with his pastor and the two of them had prayed for God's forgiveness. However, Blaine did not feel forgiven. Every day he was plagued with guilt and was losing his grip on reality. It was affecting every facet of his life.

Drawing on a concept I learned from Bruce Narramore,[5] I asked Blaine to visualize himself at the altar of his church following a Sunday night service. He was to see himself there confessing his sin to God and proclaiming his faith in the Sonship of Jesus Christ. Then I asked him to picture the scene in heaven with Jesus sitting on the throne at the right hand of the Father (Hebrews 1:13). He was to visualize Jesus pushing aside the curtain that separates the heavenly world from the earthly world and to see Him peering over the battlements high above to Blaine kneeling below. Then I urged him to hear Jesus say, "Blaine, what are you talking about?" Blaine was to answer, "The adultery I have told You about week after week." Then he was to hear Jesus respond, "My dear Blaine, I took care of that the first time you asked. What new problem do you have that needs my attention?"

All of a sudden it became clear to the young man: God had forgiven him. The problem was that Blaine had not forgiven himself. It is axiomatic: in order to experience and receive the forgiveness of God, we have to forgive ourselves. As long as we hold grudges against ourselves, there is no way for the love of God to penetrate our consciousness and set us free from self-engendered guilt.

The catharsis that Blaine experienced in my office that day, which involved many tears and much worship and praise for the completed work of salvation in his life, became evident in a subsequent session. Having forgiven himself and experienced the total forgiveness of God and his wife, Blaine started to make a new life for them. Since they were facing their ninth wedding anniversary, they decided to ask their pastor to marry them again—with a new set of rings and with their children in attendance—and begin a relationship as though the adulterous episode had never happened. It was a dramatic gesture, and totally Blaine's idea, but it illustrates the new beginning that a man can experience when he has completely surrendered his life to Christ and accepted the unconditional forgiveness of a loving God.

Becoming a Forgiving Person

There is another side of forgiveness that a man must also learn, and that is how to handle situations when he has been sinned against. This is when he has been the victim of an injustice rather than being the one who inflicted pain. Since it is the nature of Christ to be forgiving, a man's capacity to forgive other people is a reflection of the nature of Christ that is being developed in the human personality.

Jan didn't like me. Neither did she appreciate the psychology class I was teaching and she was required to attend. She chose to sit on the front row and read her Bible while I was lecturing on psychology and Christian faith. It was getting to me and I was having difficulty ignoring her distracting behavior. I made it a matter of prayer, searching my heart to see if I had done anything to offend her and trying to understand her motivation. Then I prayed for the Lord to intervene in His own way to change either my attitude or Jan's.

The following week I noticed that Jan was absent from class. That was unusual because she was very regular in attendance. Later that morning I was sitting in my office and saw her hobble down the hall to the post office. As she came back by my door her leg buckled, and she collapsed on the floor. I jumped up and offered assistance, helping her into a chair in my office. Embarrassed, she told me that she had been studying in her apartment and her leg had gone to sleep. Not realizing it, she stood up and her knee turned the wrong way, spraining a tendon with very painful results.

At that moment I was concentrating on Jan's need, not our differences. So I asked her if she wanted me to pray for her and help her to her car. "Yes," was the response. The prayer was short and simple but the results were dramatic. Jan got up out of the chair and walked out of the office without a limp and was back in class the next day. But this time she had her textbook in front of her and was taking notes. Nothing more was said about the incident.

It was a couple of years later, when I was teaching on another campus and Jan was involved in Christian service, that I saw her standing outside the door of my lecture hall. When I dismissed the class I walked out to greet her. She had a very serious look on her face. Before I could finish a polite greeting she interrupted me with: "God told me I would never have His touch on my ministry until I came and asked you to forgive me of the way I acted in your psychology class." "I already have, a long time ago," I said as I embraced her. I felt the tension flow out of her body as she responded to my embrace. At that moment we both recognized the power of forgiveness.

To forgive is to treat the other person as though the infraction never occurred. Paul put it this way: "Forbearing one another, if any man have a quarrel against any; even as Christ forgave you, so also do ye" (Colossians 3:13). H. Norman Wright suggests that it is easier to look at what forgiveness is *not* before looking at what it is. He says, "Forgiveness is not forgetting. God constructed us in such a way that our brain is like a giant computer. Whatever has happened to us is stored in our memory. The remembrance will always be with us."[6]

But, Wright points out, there are two ways of remembering. One is to recall the offense as historical information that has no bearing on the present. The other is to recall with the hurt fresh and the feelings agitated. How many times have you heard someone say, "Yes, I'll forgive you but I won't forget"? He is telling you that he will continue to hold the incident against you. It is this kind of grudge that fragments relationships and keeps love from flowing.

True forgiveness is very complex. It involves remembering, but without holding a grudge or withholding trust. It is not pretending that the event never happened, for reality never lets you forget what actually occurred. Forgiveness is an act of the will—a cognitive decision, not a feeling. No one ever really feels like forgiving, but through the grace of God, through the shed blood of Jesus Christ on Calvary, the capacity to forgive is imparted to the believer.

There are also some things that a forgiving person refrains from doing, even though it would be the most natural thing in the world to do.

1. *When you forgive you do not bring up the past.* You declare a moratorium on all that happened in the past; you leave it buried in the past and never bring it up again, even in the heat of anger.

2. *When you forgive you do not demand a change in behavior in order to prove that the forgiveness was really justified.* You recognize that forgiveness is a process and that it takes time for the sinful habit that caused the problem in the first place to be altered. You have heard it said, as I have: "I'll forgive you this time, but don't ever let it happen again. If you do, I'll leave you and never come back."

3. *When you forgive you run the risk of being hurt again.* But that is what forgiveness is all about: it involves vulnerability, loving enough to trust yourself and the other person in a new relationship.

4. *When you forgive you stop justifying your own behavior.* You do not excuse your spontaneous or planned reaction to the hurt.

5. *When you forgive you do not seek revenge.* That responsibility lies only with the Lord, and it will always be from an eternal perspective.

What happens when you don't forgive? Bitterness is the result. Christians are encouraged to "Follow peace with all man, and holiness, without which no man shall see the Lord, looking diligently lest any man fail of the grace of God, lest any root of bitterness springing up trouble you, and by it many be defiled" (Hebrews 12:14,15). Bitterness is like a poison that leads to psychosomatic illness—physical ills that are caused by wrong thinking (peptic ulcers, colitis, hypertension, migraine headaches, lower back pains, chest pains, and certain forms of asthma and arthritis).

No one, not even Biblical writers, claim that forgiveness is easy. However, it is essential to living the kind of life that brings the blessing of God and allows the free operation of His Holy Spirit in our lives.

David Augsburger puts it succinctly:

> Forgiving is self-giving with no self-seeking. It gives love where the enemy deserves bondage. It gives understanding where the enemy deserves punishment. It gives understanding where the enemy anticipates anger and revenge. Forgiveness refuses to seek its own advantage. It gives back to the other person his freedom and his future.[7]

St. Francis of Assisi was the son of a wealthy merchant family. He was known for his highly competitive nature. After his encounter with Christ he demonstrated the freedom that comes from actualizing in Christ and becoming a forgiving person. Nowhere in literature is there a better picture of a masculine personality freed from compulsive competition through divine forgiveness than is reflected in his historic prayer:

> Lord, make me an instrument of Thy peace. Where there is hatred, let me sow love; where there is injury, pardon; where there is doubt, faith; where there is despair, hope; where there is sadness, joy; where there is darkness, light.

> O Divine Master, grant that I may not so much seek to be consoled, as to console; not so much to be understood, as to understand; not so much to be loved, as to love. For it is in giving that we receive, it is in pardoning that we are pardoned, it is in dying that we are born again to eternal life.[8]

Notes

1. Erik H. Erikson, *Identity: Youth and Crisis* (New York: W. W. Norton and Company, Inc., 1968).
2. Ibid., pp. 123-24.
3. Walt Menninger, *Happiness Without Sex* (Kansas City: Sheed Andrews and McMeel, Inc., 1976).
4. Erickson, *Identity,* p. 138.
5. Bruce Narramore and Bill Counts, *Guilt and Freedom* (Santa Ana, CA: Vision House Publishers, 1974).
6. H. Norman Wright, *The Pillars of Marriage* (Glendale: Gospel Light Publications, 1979), p. 162.
7. David Augsburger, *70 × 7: The Spirit of Forgiveness* (Chicago: Moody Press, 1970), p. 40.
8. Alan Paton, *Instrument of Thy Peace* (New York: The Seabury Press, 1978), p. 9.

Chapter 6
The Male Emotions

Herb Goldberg, in *The Hazards of Being Male,* describes what for him is "the feeling bind": throughout his life, if he expresses his feelings openly and readily cries, screams, behaves sensually, etc., he may be viewed as "unstable" or "neurotic." If he controls his feelings carefully he will inevitably become guarded, hidden, and emotionally unknown to himself and other people and viewed as "cold" and even hostile. *Either way he loses:* if he lets it all hang out, he is considered to be immature and to lack self-control. If he contains his emotions he's considered secretive, distant, and overly self-controlled.[1]

On the one hand, modern literature is commanding that men emote! On the other hand, we are still telling our young boys not to cry unless they have *good reason,* not to be fearful of anything lest they be labeled "chicken," "scaredy-cat," or "gutless." We men are in a real bind as to what to do with our emotions.

DEPENDENCY

A boy who clings to his parents is an embarrassment. He is encouraged from a very young age to cut the apron strings. In some ways this is healthy and constructive in a society where independence is encouraged. Over the years men have probably learned to fend for themselves more readily than have women. Yet this is a double-edged sword. Because boys are so heavily discouraged from any signs of dependency, even normal feelings of wanting to lean on other people are suppressed. The result is a mistrust of others. The man's needs are bottled up and disowned. He is unable to put himself in the hands of another person, unwilling to trust an associate to follow through on a work assignment.

With feelings of dependence suppressed, a man may not ever allow himself to become intimate. He cannot put himself in so vulnerable a position. He must be ready at a moment's notice to be on his own and independent.

PASSIVITY

Along with a taboo upon the expression of dependency comes a strong restriction on passivity. A man is aggressive, not passive. An aggressive animal cannot rest. He must be the initiator at all times, especially with a woman. Go, go, go! Push! Push! Accomplish! There is no permission for rest and recovery. If a male is passive for a moment, he may be labeled weak or "feminine." Even God with all His potency and power rested on the seventh day of His creation!

ASKING FOR HELP

Tied in with the extreme resistance to admitting feelings of passivity and dependency is the unwillingness to ask for help. I wonder how often it occurs that in looking for a particular address a man will drive around lost for a half hour, struggling on his own to find the right direction. A woman, on the other hand, does not lose pride in asking someone for help. She will ask someone each block of the way if she has to.

If a marriage is in trouble, more often than not a man will hold out until the very last days of the relationship before consenting to see a marriage counselor. Manly pride keeps us from asking the neighbor to help us figure out how to remove the fuel pump or remove the garbage disposal, lest everyone think we are dependent upon another person's help. We have already spoken about how long a man tends to put off seeing a physician for a physical illness.

Then, finally, in midlife crisis a man decides that no one

cares, that people do not respond to his needs. He decides to leave home because this new young body he has met can anticipate all of his needs just like his wife had done at first. But has that same man stated his needs throughout those 15 years of family life? Or has he instead expected others to be mind readers? Probably! Does he realize that he is now in a new relationship that will take the same course as the first one? Statistics show that second marriages work out no better than first marriages. What has to change is *the relationship in the first marriage.* For one thing, the man must begin telling his family members what he needs, what he desires, and where he hurts. He must learn how to ask for help.

As a man, I struggle with this area myself. One Sunday afternoon, about a year ago, my wife's father and his new wife were getting ready to depart for Iowa after they had visited us for a week. Karen's mother had died three years before and her father had remarried. Just as Clarence and Gladys were getting ready to leave, Cory, our oldest son, disappeared into the family room, where he was watching TV. I became annoyed with Cory, demanding that he come outside immediately to say goodbye to his grandpa. At that point Cory broke down in tears. Initially I misinterpreted those tears as his irritation over not being able to watch television. But later Cory came out with what was really behind the crying. He lamented, "Dad, will I ever see grandpa again? Dad, will grandpa go to heaven like grandma did last year? Dad, I'd really be sad if he did." With that he continued to sob for awhile. He was asking for support, and I just rocked him in my arms.

All of a sudden Cory's weeping triggered some grief reactions in Karen, and she began to cry also. Finally, after I had comforted both of them, I began to realize some of my own sad feelings. That week had been a particularly heavy one at the office. I had seen some 40 people in therapy and was feeling a burden of having given and given. Now I was also supporting my family, and I finally broke down. I shared with Karen *my* need at that point, stating how alone and burdened I had felt all week. I asked for help.

Notice that I was the last one to do so. But I did. And much support was forthcoming. What if I had continued to hold in those feelings? I might have felt rejection, resentment, and anger. I would have reinforced my own notion that I must never ask for help: "I've got to handle it all by myself." How long can you go on handling life by yourself? How long before you reach a crisis?

Ken Olson sums up this feeling very well:

There it is again!
A twinge of pain?
Forget it. It will go away.
In the business of my day.
I've places to go and things to do . . .
A round of meetings with entrepreneurs.
Planes to catch and taxis to hail,
I have life by the tail.
But what is this painful wail?
From the depths of me I ache.
It greets me when I wake.
Even in a crowded room of people
I can hear a haunting toll from a church bell steeple.
There's nothing wrong with me.
I'm a success, as anyone can see.
I — I hurt. I feel an emptiness.
This feeling, is it loneliness?
Loneliness?
I'm married with children, three.
Yet at times I feel so alone.
Maybe it's time to come down from my throne.
It's not good for a man to be alone.[2]

FEAR

A man is not to show fear. He can feel it, but *never* is he to let on that he is fearful. "Big boys don't cry." We spend a lifetime, as men, proving that we are courageous, foolhardy, full of risk. We climb mountains, ride motorcycles, jump out of airplanes. Whatever it takes to prove that we are without fright, we do. For if a man were to be discovered with any fear in him he would, by definition, not be a man. He then automatically becomes weak, feminine, "yellow," not trustworthy, and even sexually unattractive.

And a woman can reinforce this notion by believing that "any man who shows fear *makes me* insecure" or by ignoring or shutting off any expressed fears.

Certainly it is a real plus to move through life without undue fear. Proverbs 14:30 tells us, "A tranquil mind gives life to the flesh" (RSV). Isaiah 43:1 states, "Fear not, for I have redeemed you; I have called you by name, and you are mine" (RSV). My point here is not to suggest that men should be worrywarts. Not at all. What I am saying is that a man should have the *option* of expressing fear. When Jesus was in the Garden of Gethsemane literally sweating over his impending death, He pleaded with His heavenly Father, "Please take this cup from me." And to His disciples He stated, "My soul is very sorrowful, even to death; remain here and watch with me." Those are the words of man who was dreading something, the words of a man who needed His friends for reassurance and support. In this passage, I believe that Jesus was modeling for us men that it is okay to express fear, even in the presence of other men.

SADNESS AND TEARS

If a woman cries people comfort her. If a man cries people usually are offended and want to turn away or do something to stop the tears as soon as possible. There can even be a disgust shown toward a man crying because it indicates that he is unable to control himself.

Four years ago Karen's mother, Myrt, died of lymphoma cancer. It had been a hard, bitter, and sad struggle for the entire family. Karen called me from Iowa, where she had been staying with Myrt during her last days. It was just a bit after midnight on my birthday when the phone rang, and I knew what Karen would say the moment I answered: "Mom died, Jerry! Mom died." And then many tears were shed.

I slept a couple of hours, hopped in the car, and began the 750-mile trip to Iowa. Karen had asked me to say something at the funeral, so I prepared what I would say while I wept in the car off and on all day. I can remember thinking, "If I just hold myself together and not shed too many tears I'll be a real strength to everyone." When I arrived at the Lambert homestead, Karen's father came running out to meet me. Never before had we embraced, but at that moment we did, while tears of sadness rolled from our eyes.

I can remember walking up to Myrt's bedroom with Karen and saying, "I could just bawl my heart out." Karen replied, "Please do—I'd feel so much better." She was saying, in effect, "If you grieve over my mom's death, I'll know that you really cared for her." With that bit of permission I let loose a second time.

But at the funeral itself I just knew I could not let anyone down. I had to be strong. I had to do a "professional job" and get through my part of the service. These were my in-laws, and I couldn't "let them down."

From the second I walked onto the platform I felt sadness and tears welling up inside me. The minister gave some opening remarks and then it was time for me to give the obituary and a few personal remarks. I walked to the pulpit, took a deep breath, uttered one sentence, and lost it. I began to weep. Apparently the Lord did not have in mind that I should be in control. No matter how hard I tried to fight back the tears, they burst forth. In fact the harder I tried to hold back, the more readily they flowed. As I looked out over the pews in that little church, those tough rural men were tearing up from one end of the sanctuary to the other.

At that moment it occurred to me that the Lord didn't want me to control my emotions. He wanted me to let go of them. For if the professional psychologist could lose it, perhaps that meant that the other men who were mourning could lose it also. Then all of a sudden I felt a mighty surge of strength well up inside me and I gave a very hopeful talk about Myrt's life and God's promises. Again, it was as if God were in control and said, "Okay, you've shown your sadness; now give them some hope." I don't believe I will ever forget the meaning I received from the events surrounding Myrt's death. I have feelings! If I express my feelings maybe others can feel freer to express their feelings. I don't have to always be in control, even if I am a man! Hey, man, open up and live! Don't lock yourself up in a closet. Give yourself; give the gift of your emotions to another person.

HURT

Hurt, fear, and sadness are probably the toughest emotions for a man to express. What often happens with all three of these feelings is that they are either suppressed consciously or repressed unconsciously. Over time these emotions, especially hurt, turn into anger and revengefulness. The first emotion to be felt is *hurt*. Perhaps your wife has said something negative about you at a party, which embarrasses you. You are really hurt and feel cut down by her remark. But, so that she doesn't see you as a weak person, you don't let her know how much pain this incident has caused you. Instead, you later really let her have it. You unleash *anger*, which is now the second emotion to be felt. She becomes defensive in response to your anger, and you feel even more hurt because she does not understand how humiliated and annihilated you felt. Then you begin to suppress the anger and there is a building up of *revengefulness,* the third emotion to be felt. You might begin to sense a need to get even. "If she can't understand my hurt or anger over what she did, maybe if she's on the receiving end she'll know what I mean."

And now think of this cycle going on with several events per week, and you've built up quite a storehouse of revengefulness. What needs to be expressed is the *original hurt.* If this were done, anger and revenge would be less likely. Women may also need to tune into and not deny men's "weak" feelings.

Sometimes the three feelings can occur within seconds. When you experience emotional or physical hurt, the response quickly turns to anger. The intensity and awareness of hurt feelings can accelerate rapidly seconds after the event that caused them. The anger quickly begins to grow more intense. This feeling peaks out above the emotion of hurt in just a few seconds and then the third response occurs—the desire to hurt or get revenge. If this lingers it turns to bitterness or resentment, which may hurt the one with the feelings more than the person it is against. [3]

ANGER

How do you express anger toward other people? Jim Clark, as husband and father, expressed it this way:

When I come home from work I just want to be alone. I've been putting out brush fires all day and the first thing my wife hits me with is, "The kids have been horrible all day long!" I ask her, does she expect me to do everything? Can't I have *any* peace? Just leave me alone. I'm in no mood for solving problems. Can't you handle your own problems with the kids? After all, you don't exactly help me solve *my* problems. All *I* do is bring home the bacon and you spend it. Can't you keep things on an even keel here at home?

Then there's an argument. Or perhaps my wife starts crying. I just can't handle tears, so I either get angry and leave or I blow up. (I feel hurt and sorry inside, but I won't let her know.) After the initial blowup I retreat. Now I'm feeling completely misunderstood, frustrated, and angry. But I will not risk expressing it again. Women just don't understand. At this point I feel so lonely and full of pain!

Why is it that anger is misunderstood? How does it happen that the expression of anger is so difficult? Is it wrong to express this emotion? Whom can you express it toward? How? Some of these questions will be discussed in ensuing chapters. But let's take a look at a few of the questions now.

Why is it that anger is misunderstood? First, because the anger expressed may be a cover for fear, hurt, or frustration. It may very well be that Jim Clark is hurt by the nonsupport he is receiving at work. Perhaps he has stuck his neck out for a colleague and received no thanks. Or perhaps he has pulled off a creative effort but his boss has not noticed it. On top of the hurt may be some real fear inside Jim that he is not an adequate father. There's been little time of late to be with the kids. Also, there may be a real frustration with this lack of time for what Jim keenly feels is more important. Then, at the moment when his wife hits him with "the kids have been horrible," the *hurt, fear,* and *frustration* come out disguised and in a gush of emotion.

The feeling that is available to the consciousness is *anger* instead of hurt, fear, or frustration. Jim's wife doesn't get a chance to hear what Jim is *really* feeling, but instead she experiences him as attacking her. What Jim needs to do is to sort out his *primary* feelings and express these.

A second reason that Jim's feelings were not understood was that his wife, Susan, had a few feelings of her own. And he did nothing to let her know he heard them. He did not validate her feelings by saying, "Honey, I can see you've had a frustrating day at best!" When *my* feelings are validated by someone, I feel appreciated. I feel understood and I want to *understand back*. So there's a little gem of truth here, I believe. *If you want to be understood, listened to, or appreciated, then understand, listen, and appreciate first.*

A third cause of Jim's being misunderstood was that Susan did not validate Jim's feelings. If she had said, "You sound really bent out of shape today," Jim would have been invited to explore his feelings more fully. In fact, if Jim and Susan had posed a listening stance with each other for just five minutes, chances are that Jim's frustration and hurt would have been brought to the fore. In addition, Susan was probably sitting on some fears and frustrations of her own that had nothing to do with her relationship with Jim. But instead, in haste and a nonlistening posture, their real feelings had been squelched, buried, disguised, and used against each other in about 30 seconds!

Notice that in answering the question "Why wasn't Jim's anger understood?" we discussed basically two reasons: 1) the actual feelings were not expressed clearly, and 2) they were not validated or listened to. In the next chapter we will discuss in detail the nuts and bolts of these two critical factors in dealing with emotions. The two critical factors again are: 1) listening to feelings, and 2) expressing feelings *clearly*.

Why is the expression of anger so difficult? You might answer quickly, "Because Christians should not express anger. It's a sin!" Certainly the Bible condemns explosive anger. In fact, this type of anger is mentioned a total of 20 times, in such passages as Ephesians 4:31 and Galatians 5:20. We are instructed to control explosive anger. Scripture also argues against provoking other people to anger. This resulting anger is often in the form of irritation, exasperation, and embitterment. A third type of anger mentioned is a simmering type of anger, which feeds on itself and is constantly smoldering, ready to ignite at any second. This kind can be likened to an enduring resentment that hangs on for days or years. Again, we are told to refrain from this type of anger.

Yet in Ephesians 4:26 we are told, "Be angry and sin not." Here the type of anger discussed is legitimate. Mark 3:5 records Jesus as having looked upon the Pharisees with anger. According to H. Norman Wright the word "anger" in these two verses means an abiding and sealed habit of the mind which is aroused under certain conditions against evil or injustice. This is the type of anger that Christians are encouraged to have—the anger that includes no revenge. You are aware of this kind of anger, and it is under control. Your reasoning powers are involved, and when reason is present, anger such as this is proper. The Scriptures not only permit it but on some occasions even demand it! Perhaps this sounds strange to some people who have thought for years that all anger is wrong. But the Word of God does state that *we are to be angry!*[4] In the next chapter we will discuss how to do this Biblically.

Another reason that it is difficult to express anger is that we have never learned how to do so properly. Recently a middle-aged woman told me, "I just can't get angry." That statement led us to a discussion of the type of parental models she had in expressing anger. Her father never showed anger until he became so explosive that he broke out windows or threw tools at the walls. Her mother was a peacemaker who would impose extreme guilt trips for any expression of anger. My client had never seen the healthy, appropriate expression of anger. The result was that she either sat on anger completely or exploded into some nasty displays of it. Thus she had evidence for herself as to why she should feel guilty for expressing anger!

Some men sense that if they were to express irritation they would completely lose control and fly into a rage. So they fulfill that prophecy by allowing anger to build up daily until some innocent event blows the cork off the bottle of stored up anger, and rage bursts forth.

Fear of rejection is a fourth reason why people have difficulty in expressing anger. If I express some irritation with you, you may become defensive toward me. You may reject our friendship. You may put up a wall between us. You may misunderstand the intensity of my anger or the intent behind my words. And the more fragile my own ego, the greater is the chance that I'll feel obliterated by your negative response. This is part of the "nice guy" syndrome. If I'm nice to all people at all times, no one will reject me. If no one ever rejects me, my own self-esteem will be intact. But will it really? How much energy does it take to please everyone all the time? How do you really feel about yourself if you're that careful about your own opinions, needs, and convictions? And what's your opinion of the Mr. Nice Guy type who never expresses *anything* contrary to popular opinion?

"IRRATIONAL" BEHAVIOR

Time after time in marriage counseling I have observed a highly rational male with his emotional counterpart acting out this little scenario:

Husband: "If you really thought this through, dear, you wouldn't feel that way."

Wife: (Tearfully) "Oh, there you go again with your logic."

Husband: "Well, one of us has to."

Wife: "I have a mind too, you know."

Husband: (Thinking, "If she'd only use it!")

From a cognitive point of view, men are programmed to be thinkers and problem-solvers, to be analytical, scientific, and objective. In the scientific, technical, mechanical world we live in, these qualities have become absolutely vital. When an engineer designs a bridge, you want to know how strong it will be and how long it will last. It isn't too important to know how the engineer "feels" about the bridge, because that doesn't answer the question that needs to be answered. The world of science and technology demands accuracy and people who can be precise. And many men have the gift of analytical logic, which is critical in human relationships as well.

Yet if we become too caught up in the rational, we keep ourselves shut out from the emotional. If we are only logical, we begin to sound like Mr. Spock, giving monotone output on emotion-laden issues. We become computerlike, unaware of the heartbeat of another person, unaware of our own pain and joy. We cut ourselves off from the intuitive part of life, the part that asks, "How do you feel?" or "What's the most important part of your life right now?" or "What are your dreams for the future?" or "You seem a little down . . . is something wrong?"

Why is it that with so many men alcohol becomes a vehicle for the expression of emotion? Why is it that men "let their hair down" when drinking with the boys—telling dirty jokes and watching porno films—but can't express absolute delight or weep bitterly? Why do men dream of wild women, of chucking their present lifestyles, and of going fishing with the gang? Perhaps part of the answer lies in a need that a man has—a need to be irrational, to think with his heart.

In his inspiring book *Barefoot Days of the Soul,* Maxie Dunnam expresses the "irrational," intuitive, feeling side of life. He says that awareness, spontaneity, and intimacy, in the context of our commitment to Christ, are the characteristics of living in joy this new day.

Awareness

Knowing what is happening now
tuned-in to the moment
appreciating the world around you
listening to what others are saying
feeling the wind

or the mist
or the fog
seeing the sunset
or the lake
or the snowflake
or the butterfly
sensing the meaning of
the smile
or tear
or angry shout
or withdrawal
or attack
or silence
being in touch with self
feeling awe
mystery
loneliness
sorrow
pain
tenseness
oneness with others
oneness with nature
feeling separated from self
from others
from nature

Spontaneity

flexible
not locked into yesterday
or to the expectations of others
liberated
to be a "fool"
a "fool for Christ"
from a predetermined life-style
to explore new ways

      of thinking
      feeling
      responding
    to reevaluate and change
free
    to decide for self
    to outwit fate
    to fail
    to be wrong
open
    to God's bidding
    to God's action
    to the kingdom within.

Intimacy

open to others
willing to risk friendship
    to express love and affection
willing to be honest
    to let go
    and reveal self
respect others'
    inability to share
does not "force" intimacy
or invade privacy
lives with others in the here and now
sees others in their uniqueness
    and affirms that uniqueness
    by relating to it.[5]

In each of the experiences described in Dunnam's verse, there is an irrational element, an element that steps out in risk, in faith! It's not that we are to step out completely oblivious to reason and to live the "if it feels good, do it" philosophy. But in order to respond to life, we simply must respond to emotion, within us and within others.

Notes

1. Herb Goldberg, *The Hazards of Being Male* (New York: Signet, 1976), p. 88.
2. Ken Olson, *Hey Man! Open Up and Live* (New York: Fawcett, 1978), pp. 147-48.
3. H. Norman Wright, *The Family That Listens* (Wheaton: Victor Books, 1978).
4. H. Norman Wright, *An Answer to Anger and Frustration* (Eugene, OR: Harvest House, 1977).
5. Maxie Dunnam, *Barefoot Days of the Soul* (Waco: Word Books, 1975).

Chapter 7
Expressions of Emotion

The biggest complaint that a wife has about her husband is that he doesn't talk to her enough. A man's biggest complaint about his wife is that she doesn't want to have sex often enough. As Ken Olson has stated, these two fundamental needs are related to each other. Not enough discourse leads to less intercourse.[1]

Before marriage there is much to talk about. In fact, the man may tend to be a real chatterbox. Or perhaps the woman sees her spouse-to-be as the strong, silent type who "really has something to say" on the few occasions when he opens up. Besides, she'll have her whole life to change him. And even after the wedding there may be a good deal of verbiage coming from his knowledgeable tongue. Yet gradually he becomes less and less communicative. Fewer and fewer stories from work are brought home. And now when she asks him, "How was work, honey?" he mumbles an "Okay" and slides quietly up the stairs to take a shower and change clothes. She begins to bring this up, and at first he comes up with, "I'm just tired when I come home. I need to be left alone." So she waits for an hour before she begins conversation again. This time he's camped out in front of the television watching the news and sucking on a martini. Then she just plain becomes angry: "Why can't you *ever* talk to me?" He retreats even further or becomes defensive.

Then one night they're out with another couple, and she sees the wittiness and interesting chitchat come back. The only problem is that it's with the other guy's wife. She asks, "Why doesn't he talk to me like that anymore?" Let's look at some possible answers.

EMOTIONAL VERSUS FACTUAL COMMUNICATORS

One of the clearest differences I see between men and women is that men *tend* to be factual communicators and women *tend* toward emotional discourse. Let's compare emotional communication with factual communication. Dr. Ross Campbell has described these two patterns:

> We can start by realizing that there is a difference between cognitive (that is, intellectual or rational) communications and emotional (that is, feeling) communications. Persons who communicate primarily on a cognitive level deal mainly with factual data. They like to talk about such topics as sports, the stock market, money, houses, jobs, etc., keeping the subject of conversation out of the emotional area.[2]

When the husband comes home from work he may talk about the facts only: "We signed the new contract today." His wife asks, "How did it go?" He replies, "Oh, fine, just fine," meaning, "The contract did get signed." Meanwhile, however, he is leaving out the frustration of six hours of negotiation, disagreements, and fear that he experienced in fighting for his position. She assumes that everything is fine emotionally, whereas all that's really fine is that the contract did get signed. And that may be all that is important to him at this point. Later all his frustration and fear are channeled into a tennis game, a football game, or a bombastic tirade about the messy house. Concurrently, his wife is wondering why he doesn't talk anymore. It's partly because he leaves out a good share of the emotional area. All she hears are "boring," straightforward facts.

Perhaps she communicates more on the feeling level. It could be that she tires easily of purely factual data, and feels a need to share feelings, especially with her spouse. She probably feels that the atmosphere between husband and wife must be as free as possible from unpleasant feelings such as tension, anger, and resentment. So of course she will want to talk about these emotional things, resolve conflicts, clear the air, and keep things pleasant. At this point he may avoid talking about feelings, and so we have the "nag" situation staged perfectly. She says, "You *never* talk about your feelings." He retorts, "Just leave me alone." And finally she does!

Are you more emotional or cognitive? Is it easier for you to talk about feelings or facts? A person who is more emotional is not less intelligent. And a person who is inclined more toward the cognitive has as many feelings inside as the emotional type. He just has trouble expressing them or even sometimes realizing them. But they *are* there.

THINK OUT LOUD

Many times when I see a "cognitive type" man in counseling I encourage him to think out loud. I'll say something like, "All those feelings and thoughts that you're mulling over right now I'd like for you to say out loud. Just say what you're thinking, without worrying whether it comes out right." This is a strategy you can use if you're more or less a "cognitive type." When you find yourself off in a corner, preoccupied with feelings, thoughts, and decisions, find another person and "think out loud" with him or her. Just say what's on your mind. Begin with matters that are not critical or too personal and work toward those that are.

USE THE XYZ METHOD

Let's take the "signing of the contract" example again. Let

x = the event, signing the contract

y = your feelings about the event, the process of getting the contract signed

z = the consequences of the event for you personally.

The man comes home from work and says, "We signed the new contract today." If he stops here he will have expressed the x part of xyz: the facts, the event. If he continues with y (feelings) he might add, "Wow, was that a frustrating contract to get signed! I was scared to death that they wouldn't see my arguments and that my ideas wouldn't be implemented." Then he further clarifies and expands his statement with z (consequences for his life): "If I hadn't gotten the group to sign the contract there would have been no trip over the weekend, and Monday off would have been out of the question. Wow, am I relieved. Let's celebrate!"

This is a much richer message than merely "We signed the new contract" and "Everything went fine." The person on the receiving end is much more stimulated by the "xyz" message than by the mere "x" message. Furthermore, if the person on the receiving end is an "emotional type" you have just given him or her a gift—a gift of your feelings.

Use xyz as a memory device in reminding yourself to give a more complete message with both facts *and* emotions. Write the letters on your palm. Put a sign up in your car: "xyz."

KEEP A DIARY OF FEELINGS

It is no accident that the Marriage Encounter movement encourages individuals to first write down their feelings on paper and *then* talk about them. Many times in the early stages of learning to express certain feelings it is easier to write them down first. In doing this you do not have to worry about any negative feedback. You have time to express your feelings just the way you would like. You're not on the spot and are less likely to be covering yourself from possible onslaught. Thus you are more likely to be honest. This is sometimes a good way to approach touchy issues in communicating feelings. By expressing these feelings in writing first you get a second chance to express them later, with some refinements. The main idea here is to let loose on paper with exactly what you feel, because there is little risk involved, and you will have a chance to see what's inside.

LISTENING TO THE LORD

Choose a time at approximately the same hour every day when you can be fairly certain of being undisturbed for ten minutes. Sit down with pen and paper. Offer a simple prayer affirming that you have already given your whole life to Jesus Christ, and that it is your desire to be guided by Him. Tell Him you are listening and ask Him to speak to you. Then write down whatever comes to your mind. Be sure to *write*. This helps keep your mind from wandering. It gives you a record you can look back on.

Using this method for listening to the Lord has been a very rich experience for me. Through it the Lord helps me become more aware of emotions buried deep inside. He convicts me of my own selfishness and helps ready me for the expression of important issues in my life. Sometimes He reminds me to "think out loud" or "add more details" to my communications with my wife. At other times He will remind me that I haven't been honest with a friend or that I'm burying some fear or hurt. I have simply found this time of free association an invaluable part of my day. It digs up unconscious material from the depths of my being and helps me respond to the emotional feelings.

TALKING TO THE LORD

A few days ago I was really angry with a friend whom I felt had clobbered me for being honest with him. I had been up-front and assertive, and had expressed my needs to him, so he withdrew from me and our friendship. I was crushed! I was engulfed with feelings of guilt for having confronted him. I was sad and scared because I thought it was the end of our relationship. Anger also welled up inside me because I thought I had confronted him "correctly." I had used good principles of communication, had allowed him to give me feedback, and was positive in my approach. But it all backfired! I hadn't felt pain like that in some time. I felt numb, shut off from a close friend. Some thoughts entered my mind:

It does no good to confront a friend . . . anyone, for that matter. All this garbage about being honest with people is for the birds. I'll *never* confront a friend again. Yet in my counseling I encourage clients to be up-front with their intimates. Who do I think I'm kidding? God, what are You up to?

It was at this point that I began to talk to God about my dilemma. He's a great listener! He seldom interrupts, seems to accept what I say, and allows me to clarify what I'm feeling. I confessed these same feelings to the Lord in prayer, conversationally. It was a beautiful release of pent-up emotions. I just let them all hang out. I even expressed my extreme anger to God for allowing me to even express those negative feelings to my friend in the first place. Then I told God I would never risk that kind of confrontation again, that I'd resort to a life of phoniness before I'd risk losing a close friendship.

Finally, once I had gotten out all the pain inside, God allowed me to begin to think through what I would actually do. Usually we have to release the pent-up feelings before we can begin to think rationally and plan for constructive action. And, as men, especially *because* we are men, we need to confess those feelings to someone first, before we can really make decent decisions. If no one else is available (and even if someone else is), try engaging God in conversational prayer. Just talk to Him with the safe assurance that He'll keep in absolute confidence what you have to say. He won't judge your feelings. He'll allow you to express them. You don't have to be perfect for the Lord.

Once I had expressed my hurt feelings to God, I gave them to my wife and she listened also. *Then* I was able to make some decisions about what to do next. I called my friend and reconciled with him. Some of the ways I had interpreted his feedback were incorrect. He did not wish to end the relationship! He was pleased that I cared enough to call. It was reassuring to him to hear me say that I value our friendship and that I was sorry if I had hurt him.

But what gave me the freedom to call him, the freedom to stick my neck out once again? An accepting, listening heavenly Father who is always there to hear my cry, my despair. How lucky I am to have a friend in Jesus! He's one Man I can express my deepest groans to, and He will not compare me with another person nor judge me as a "failure" because I've stumbled! Maxie Dunnam states:

> Because prayer is relationship—relationship of self and God—prayer involves not only an effort to come to a deeper understanding of God, it involves a continuous quest of self-understanding. Because so many of our relationships are superficial and much of life is surface-living, our temptation is to put forth in prayer someone who is not our real self, who is a pretension. Jesus warned, "When you pray, don't be like play actors." We are not entering into vital communion with God if we remain in our "stage personality" when we come to our meeting with God.[3]

Don't be a "play actor" with God. You don't have to be. He's the one Person you can be completely open with. You are eternally significant and secure in His friendship.

DEVELOPING FRIENDSHIPS

After Christmas in 1979 I was feeling a real sense of loneliness. As I shared this emptiness with Karen, it became more apparent that what I needed was some deeper involvement with male friends. During the past year I had set my family as a priority and had somehow left out male companionship in the process. Thus, after the first week in January

1980, I began to work intentionally toward spending quality time with men I like. This meant going out to breakfast, playing racquetball and tennis, chatting on the telephone, going fishing, and a few other activities which I initiated. Some of my loneliness began to decrease. I again was sharing with and hearing an adult male perspective which I needed in order to feel completely understood. My present goal is to purposely contact at least one male friend for a conversation and/or activity each week.

Herb Goldberg admits:

> As adult males in our culture the phenomenon of being without even a single buddy or good friend is a common one—so widespread, in fact, that it is not seen as unusual nor is it even spoken about. Rather, it is taken for granted. Many men I interviewd admitted to not having one intimate male friend whom they totally trusted and confided in.[4]

In 2 Timothy 4:9-11 NIV Paul describes his loneliness and need for his friends, especially Timothy, as he writes from prison. Paul was certain that he would be killed soon, and he needed the support of his friends. Listen to his words:

> Do your best [Timothy] to come to me quickly, for Demas, because he loved this world, has deserted me and has gone to Thessalonica. Crescens has gone to Galatia, and Titus to Dalmatia. Only Luke is with me. Get Mark and bring him with you, because he is helpful to me in my ministry.

Paul was feeling lonely. He needed some support. He was expressing his needs directly. He was saying to two of his male friends, "Hey, I need you guys . . . I'm feeling deserted and alone. Other friends have left me to fight this battle on my own . . . to experience prison by myself. Please come! I need you guys!" Here is a giant of the Christian church, a man who had written much of the New Testament, saying, "Timothy, I need you!"

Do you have a Timothy? A Mark? A Luke? Do you have a male friend whom you can open up to? Someone who will keep in confidence what you say, who will listen and not condemn you, but be with you in your "prison" experience of life? Do you have a guy you can call and admit, "Hey, pal, I need to talk over some important things with you. When can we get together? I'm really hurting about something and I need a listening ear"? Are you a Luke to someone else? Do you have a few male friends that you are available to? Or are you like Demas, too caught up in the things of this world—job, productivity, dollars, achievement, success—to be with another man?

I once heard a conference speaker say, "It gives another man hope for you to reveal yourself to him." As men we tend to show only our perfect, coping sides to other males, because we are taught to handle life alone. We are taught to be competitive with other males, not giving them any clues that we're not making it, because if we do, that other male will "eat us alive." So most of us men appear to have it all together; no one dares show a weak spot lest we become open to defeat and criticism. Yet I am relieved, encouraged, and hopeful when I hear another man admit, "I'm not quite the husband I'd like to be; I'm selfish; I don't give enough of my time to my children; I'm scared to death I can't continue to support my family." That kind of statement helps me realize that I'm not alone, that I don't have to measure up to an impossible yardstick of success, that other men struggle as I do.

But in order to discover this reality I need to be open with a few other guys, willing to share, to admit that I'm weak sometimes, that I'm discouraged at times, that I'm afraid, hurt.

Do you have a Luke? Jesus had twelve "Lukes." And He was the Son of God!

Notes

1. Ken Olson, *Hey Man! Open Up and Live* (New York: Fawcett, 1978).
2. D. Ross Campbell, M.D., *How to Really Love Your Child* (Wheaton: SP Publications, 1977), pp. 19-20.
3. Maxie Dunnam, *Barefoot Days of the Soul* (Waco: Word Books, 1975) p. 82.
4. Herb Goldberg, *The Hazards of Being Male* (New York: Signet, 1976), p. 127.

Chapter 8
A Man As a Person

How can a man be all that we have implied to this point in this book? Only by coming to grips with the complexity of masculinity. He must define how he sees himself and how he chooses to be a genuine, authentic, actualizing personality. To pretend to be more is dishonest; to become less is demoralizing.

THE COMPLEXITIES OF MASCULINITY

A man is many things to many people. Each relationship takes on a different role expectation. Before we look at the integrated, whole masculine personality, we must first look at the many expectations that are incumbent on him and see how—and if—he can put these pieces of his personal puzzle together to become a complete, whole person.

Born male and placed in a body that is anatomically different from the female, man must learn to live comfortably in his body, discover his sex role identity, and accept the privileges and responsibilities that come with being born male. This must be aligned with the gender identity of being masculine and the lifestyle and feelings that go with being male and masculine at the same time. The male child who is encouraged to learn masculinity in life is more comfortable with his sex-role identity than if he is unsure of what is expected of him and what is considered appropriate behavior.

This challenge places special responsibilities on the parents of the newborn male. Some family expectations of masculinity may be at odds with the broader cultural demands. When family and cultural traditions come into conflict, an identity crisis can result. Unfortunately, there are some Western expectations of masculinity that can make the adult male callous and almost unfeeling. Parents who continually say "Boys don't cry" or "Boys don't do dishes" are teaching their sons attitudes that will collide with expectations in marriage.

It is my opinion that every boy needs to learn every job in the house. He should learn to make his own bed, clean up his own room, pick up after himself, help in meal preparation, clean up the kitchen, and help keep the whole house clean and orderly. This is just as important as learning how to take care of the lawn and shubbery and maintaining a car, cycle, or other vehicles or appliances of the family. Then, when the adult male moves out on his own and has his own "pad," he will know how to take care of himself, maintain a respectable place to live, and be a good guardian of his health. All tasks in family living should be shared by both male and female members of the family, whether young or old.

The boy who sees his father taking an active part in maintaining the orderliness of the home as well as being the principal breadwinner in the family is getting the kind of balanced picture of masculinity that Joyce Landorf talks about in her excellent book *Tough and Tender*.[1] We have already seen that it is appropriate for a man to show a variety of emotions. It is how he expresses and controls his emotionality that makes him a sensitive man and not an ogre or authoritarian despot.

DEVELOPING MALE EXPECTATIONS

In subsequent chapters we will look specifically at the roles of men as husbands and fathers. In this chapter we will concentrate on the dimension of masculinity with which the male begins life, and we will examine the widening circle of relationships that he develops.

Son

The male child is named a son at birth and is surrounded with the expectations that go with being the newest male in the family.

I shall never forget when our son, Robert, was born. He had been preceded by two girls, Cindy and Joan. It was obvious from the beginning that he would have to be treated with the same loving affection we had given the girls, but there would be different expectations as he grew up. He would think differently, respond differently to situations, and set different goals in life (probably at different ages than his sisters had done).

Nita and I have tried to love each of our children equally, but we also have discovered that we need to treat each one differently because of his or her personality and sex-role differences. Now that all three of them are adults, we are pleased with the different educational and vocational paths their lives have taken and are grateful that each has chosen a lifestyle consistent with Christian values.

I grew up as an only child. My brother and sister had died before I was born, one with membranous croup, which was prevalent shortly after World War One, and the other with diphtheria. By the time I came along my parents were very eager for another child, especially one that would carry on the family name. This expectation was more than subtle from my earliest years. I learned to work beside my mother in the kitchen, for she taught me all she would have taught my sister if she had lived. My father took me into the business when I was four and started teaching me to shine shoes and ultimately to repair shoes and run all the machinery in the shop. He taught me well enough so that in the summer following my sophomore year in high school I was able to take over the business, hire a helper, and run the shop for three months while dad convalesced from a perforated appendix (and that was in prepenicillin days). I shall never forget the thrill of taking the day's receipts to lay on the pillow beside my father's fevered head at the end of the day. I was 15 at the time.

As a son I learned work productiveness, spiritual values, and a deep desire to be a helping person, but I also enjoyed the freedom to become what I felt was God's will for my life. Although my mother has been dead for ten years, my relationship with my father, now in his eighties, is as vital and open as it was in my formative years. He is still a person in whom I can confide and whose opinion I respect, but he leaves me free to follow my own destiny.

I shall never forget when we stood by my mother's coffin, looking at her cold form. Dad looked at me and said, "Son, you have one consolation: you never did anything to put your mother where she is." For the next three years he turned to me for advice about retiring, selling his business, and then choosing a new wife. He put it this way: "My heart has enlarged to the place that I can take another woman into my life without casting a shadow on the memory of your mother." I knew he was ready for a second marriage so I responded to the invitation to perform the ceremony to marry my father to my stepmother.

Relative

The extended family must be considered as a man finds his place in the broadening circle of relationships. Siblings, uncles, aunts, cousins, and grandparents all have a part to play in defining the expectations for the growing child. Some families are very close, so close that it is difficult for the young to disengage from the family of origin as they become adult and establish independent lifestyles. Families that cling together too tightly make it difficult for the newlyweds to obey the Biblical injuctions to leave parents and cleave to each other (Genesis 2:24; Matthew 19:4-6; Ephesians 5:31).

Friend

A broadening circle of friendships develops as a boy becomes a man. Some of these are intense, intimate, and lasting. Others are casual, shallow, and ephemeral. Different levels of friendships are important at any age, but there are some that become deeply meaningful. Establishing and maintaining friendships is a major masculine role. Unfortunate is the man who has few friends and knows only shallow relationships.

Some friendships require constant cultivation or they die. Other friendships seem to span time and space, no matter how long it has been since contact was made; you seem to pick up right where you left off in your last encounter, whether by letter, phone, or visit.

Married and single men need friends of both sexes. This involves the ability to maintain relationships that are cognitive, emotional, and spiritual without physical expectations. Friendships made in dating years can be perpetuated through the married years even though each person married someone else. I shall never forget how pleased I was when a college friend of mine who had married my best girlfriend called and asked me to counsel with their adolescent child. It was a strange twist of circumstances, but I considered it a privilege to counsel with the daughter of a man who "stole my girl." And we are all still friends today simply because our relationship was just that—friendship. John Scanzoni has some helpful things to say about the processes of "friending" in his book *Love and Negotiate*.[2]

Colleague

The relationship between vocational peers brings into being the status of colleague (or associate in a professional, civil, or ecclesiastical office). These are the people we work with, both male and female. There are joys in a colleague relationship but there are also some hazards. The joys come from shared interests, desires, backgrounds, and trainings being concentrated on group problem-solving and work productiveness. The hazards lie in competition, jealousy, and the "dog-eat-dog" tenacity with which some men hold onto their positions or try to move up the status ladder with inordinate ambition.

When colleagues see themselves as equals among peers, harmony prevails and productiveness is sustained at a high level. When there are rivalries, however, the tension can become unbearable. Such are the atmospheres that breed physical ills that are stress-related. Uncorrected, these can lead to medical leaves, early retirement, or being fired.

Students of organizational behavior have noted that more people lose their jobs because of personality conflicts and the inability to get along with their colleagues than are ever terminated because of lack of skill or training. One of the tasks of manhood is to learn how to do your best at what you have chosen to do and not to interfere with the progress or productiveness of your colleagues. This does not imply that everyone will agree on every point, but it does suggest that there is strength in diversity when the differences are directed toward policy and methodology but not against a person.

Citizen

Certainly the adequate male is going to want to be a good citizen. He is going to become involved in community affairs and make his contribution to see that his town, county, state, and country are a better place in which to live. He will want to become conversant with issues facing his community and to use his energies in the civic projects that are consistent with his interests and abilities. Many men find that it is consistent with God's will for their lives to become active in government and politics. To see Christan men in high positions is thrilling because it allows spiritual values to be shared in strategic places. If the United States of America is to remain a Christian nation, it is going to have to have more Christian men and women making themselves available for public office to promote the issues that are important to them and their families.

Civic involvement begins in service clubs and professional organizations and moves on to elective offices at the local, county, state, and national level.

Christian

I have purposely held the most important dimension of masculinity till the last. There is no more important declaration that a real man can make than "I'm a Christian." To have become a child of God and joint-heir with Jesus Christ is the highest accolade that could be bestowed on any man (Romans 8:17). We will close this book by noting that Jesus was the perfect model of masculinity. It is not premature at this point, however, to note that a study of the life of Jesus Christ reveals what true masculinity is all about.

Jesus was obedient to His parents (Luke 2:48-51), wept (John 11:35), and knew how to love as a friend without romantic or erotic overtones (Luke 10:38; John 11:3,36; 13:23; 19:26). Jesus became indignant with injustice (Mark 11:15-17) but was sensitive to human need (John 4:7-26; 8:11; Luke 23:42,43). He respectfully disengaged from His family of origin (Matthew 12:46-50) but planned for His mother to be taken care of after His death (John 19:25-27). Through it all He was obedient to His heavenly Father (John 4:34; Luke 22:42) and never doubted who He was (John 14:10,11).

The man who would explore all of the dimensions of masculinity must take into account his spiritual nature. Whether we view man as body, soul, and spirit or as heart, soul, mind, and strength, we must realize that one part of us is physical and will ultimately decay and die. Another part of us will exist eternally, either in the presence of God or cast away from His presence. To know that you are a child of God, that your name is written in the Lamb's book of life, assures you a place in God's eternal kingdom (Revelation 21:27). It is a decision that no person can make for another.

No father can make it for his son. Each of us stands alone before God and is accountable for whether or not we have accepted Christ as Lord (Romans 6:23). The earlier this choice is made, the happier and less complicated life will be because the Word of God and the witness of the Holy Spirit are avilable to lead the Christian man into all the truth that the Father has to share with mankind (John 16:13-15; 1 Corinthians 2:9-16).

FLEXIBILITY IN ROLE EXPECTATIONS

To try to fulfill all the roles of masculinity we have just explored would become a heavy weight on a man who felt compelled to concentrate on all of them at once. Fortunately, the Christian expectation is the only one that is a constant part of everyday life. The other roles weave in and out of life as they become of primary importance, depending on the time and the setting. Flexibility, the ability to change roles easily, is essential in keeping the balance demanded by the complexity of masculine expectations.

Rex came to me for counseling. I asked him, "What did you want to talk about?" He said, "Your daughter." I knew that he had been seeing my elder daughter for some time and assumed that this conversation might be more than academic, so I asked, "Which hat do you want me to wear—my counselor's hat or my father's hat?" He responded, "Let's try the counselor's hat first." So we did.

Near the end of the session I altered the structure of the counseling session by saying, "Now let me take off my counselor's hat and put on my father's hat and give you some information about my daughter." At that point I became very directive. I answered specific questions on a man-to-man level. The session proved to be profitable for Rex and he was able to redefine his relationship with my daughter.

Flexibility in role portrayal in no way suggests blind decision-making or trial-and-error behavior. Flexibility has a plan, but it is not so rigid that it cannot be adjusted when necessary. We are all familiar with the fact that a slight adjustment at the space propulsion laboratory can change the altitude of a rocket and head it more accurately toward a target. This is what flexibility permits in masculine behavior.

To be able to assess the total situation in which we are involved and make corrective adjustments in behavior and goals is to lead us to more responsible living. The personality that is rigid or inflexible or insists on maintaining the status quo is one that becomes miserable and makes other people unhappy. In the family, inflexibility can fragment relationships and be divisive to the togetherness that Christian family living implies.

Flexibility in fulfilling masculine expectations allows a man to focus his full attention on an immediate situation. It allows him to concentrate on an individual or group, as the case may be, without losing sight of overarching goals that are bigger than the immediate situation. With flexibility comes a freedom of choice that avoids erratic behavior or oppressive demands on other people to conform.

A special time when flexibility is essential is when making the transition from work to home. It is essential for a man to shift gears after leaving the job and to free himself from the emotional entanglements that may have put stress on his emotions. He needs to be free to face new challenges that are inevitable when he walks into the door of his home.

How well I remember the day when our middle child (Joan) caught me at the door when I arrived home from a hard day at school. I was rather abrupt in responding to her. She squared her shoulders, stood between me and the door to the bedroom where I was headed, and said, "Daddy, that's not fair. You have used all your energy on the kids at school today and you haven't saved any for us." She was right! I have had to learn to shift gears between school and home in order to be the kind of father I need to be.

The family must come before the vocation in God's order of priorities. I have had to develop strategies that will allow me to be both father and teacher, but not at the same time or in the same place. I have to allow an adequate distribution of my psychic energy so that I can do both jobs acceptably and in their proper order.

Role flexibility requires learning how to develop a number of coping skills.

Anxiety

Any situation with an unknown element in it is marked by anxiety. Anxiety has been defined as a free-floating sense of uneasiness, a feeling that all is not well, without knowing what is wrong. If the cause of the tension is known, it is usually in the form of fear or a phobia. Since anxiety is more unconscious than conscious, it is hard to put a finger on the origin of the feeling.

You wake up in the morning with a sense if dis-ease, but you don't know why. It could relate to something you dreamed, something you were thinking about before you went to bed, or something you are not looking forward to in the approaching day. Anxiety is a most common feeling. When it becomes pronounced, it leads to behavior disorders classified as neurotic and a whole series of defense mechanisms which people use to lower their anxiety as they try to cope with the affairs of everyday life.

One of the best ways I know of dealing with anxiety is to end each day with a time of prayer and Bible reading. Closing out a day that has been racked with tensions and anxieties is not easy. You need to prepare your mind for peaceful sleep. You can even influence what you will dream about. Winding your day down devotionally is a marvelous way of reducing anxiety.

Another good habit is to start the day on a spiritual note. Before you put your foot on the floor in the morning, stretch to the full length of your bed and say, "This is the day which the Lord hath made"—just for me! "I will rejoice and be glad in it" (Psalm 118:24). Personalize the affirmation. You have a right to put your name in place of the pronoun because this is your promise for a day in which you have placed the Lord in charge.

When you get up in the morning, go to the first mirror you can find and look at yourself. You may not like what you see, disheveled as you will be from a night of sleeping. But declare to yourself: "Jesus loves you." At that point He may be the only One who can, but He really does, so affirm it.

After you have completed getting yourself ready for the day—doing the best you can with what you have to work with—smile broadly and say to yourself: "And I love you too!" When you prepare to leave your room with the assurance that God loves you and you love yourself, you are ready to meet other members of your household and people on the job with a spark of happiness that will anticipate the normal tensions of the workaday world.

Conflict

Conflict is a major factor in decision-making. You are moving along nicely on a line of thought or course of action when you discover that there is a fork in the road. You cannot proceed as you have been; you must make a decision and alter the direction of your forward movement. Do you go right? Do you go left? You must make a choice. To refuse to make a choice brings about the indecisiveness of decidophobia (fear of making choices) and it surrenders to other people the right to make the choice for you. You will have surrendered your freedom of choice.

Conflicts are basically of three types:

1. *Approach-Approach*. These conflicts are those in which both options are positive and you would enjoy doing both. But you must choose between them because you can do only one thing at a time. The single male faces a conflict when there are two young ladies he is interested in dating but can't decide which one to ask out first. Certainly he can't take them both out at the same time!

2. *Avoidance-avoidance.* This kind of conflict situation arises when both options are negative, something you would rather avoid if you could. Do you study for the final exam or do you fix the flat tire on your car so you won't be late to work in a couple of hours?

3. *Approach-avoidance.* This complicated kind of conflict really heightens anxiety. There are both positive and negative elements in either choice you make. This was illustrated in counseling one day when a fellow said, "I really like this girl but I can't tolerate her mother. I asked Sherry to marry me but told her I would be taking a job out of state. She said she loved me but she was not willing to move that far from her parents because they were expecting her to take care of them in their old age."

Frustration

Frustration is like running into a brick wall. It is when your forward movement has been blocked and there is no room for change of direction to avoid the issue. Life has just told you no. What do you do when life says no? You do have options.

1. *Apathy.* The first response to frustration is apathy, the temptation to surrender, to quit trying, to give up. This leads to the uninvolvement in life that we called alienation in Chapter 3. It is emotional suicide.

2. *Withdrawal.* Another option when facing frustration is to withdraw from the scene of the conflict. This can become a habit, leading you to run from every tense situation. It leads to a nomadic life that is unsettled and unfulfilled. The young man who has become attracted to a young lady, only to be jilted for his best friend, frequently is tempted to withdraw, not only from that romantic fiasco but from any other relationship. So he swears off women and decides to be a loner. This response has no relationship to the gift of singleness (1 Corinthians 7); it is fear and flight from frustration that can only be self-defeating.

However, there are times when it is appropriate to retreat from a situation. Terry had come to the dissertation level of his doctorate. Unfortunately, his major professor retired and a new person was added to his committee, one who refused to approve the topic that Terry had thoroughly researched and was in the final stages of writing. Knowing that an impasse had been reached, he withdrew from the university, moved his family to another state, and candidated at another university for his degree. Before long Terry had passed a new set of comprehensives, had his dissertation approved, and was graduated with honors. The added course work at the new university broadened his field of knowledge so that he is now able to handle a variety of complex university jobs including serving as department chairman and directing thesis research.

3. *Lower your profile and work constructively for change.* A better approach to facing frustration is to refuse to give in to the temptation of apathy or flight. In so doing, you lower your profile, stop rigidly holding to your demands, and work constructively within the organization for the kinds of changes you feel are appropriate. This keeps you within the system and allows you time and space to demonstrate the validity of your position. You will still be there when the climate changes so that you can guide your ideas through the proper channels to adoption and implementation.

A new course to offer, a new product to market, a new invention to be tested—all may come to you ahead of the time when your company or institution is ready for such innovation. By sticking with your vision and allowing other people time to catch up with your foresight, you may very well be present when birth is given to your idea, and you can then enjoy the rewards of patient labor.

Outside Pressure

Anxiety, conflict, and frustration are internal pressures that stymie growth and interfere with productivity. Outside pressures also can impede progress and produce tension. Parental demands on children and young people, social demands from those in authority, educational demands by a school or vocation with rigid entrance requirements—all these add to the discomfort of men of all ages. How a man deals with these pressures, both internal and external, becomes an indication of his ability to cope and is a measure of his flexibility and adaptability. Man as a species has survived through the centuries only through adaptation. This is no less true now than it was in early times, when the first adventurers crossed the Carpathian Mountains into Central Europe or opened up the American West or Australian outback.

BECOMING A SELF-DISCIPLINED PERSON

In Chapter 12 we will look at the importance of self-discipline in the life of the mature man. At this point it is sufficient to note that discipline is the introduction of control into the life of a person. Solomon said, "He that is slow to anger is better than the mighty, and he that ruleth his spirit than he that taketh a city" (Proverbs 16:32). The Living Bible translates it this way: "It is better to be slow-tempered than famous; it is better to have self-control than to control an army."

The male who becomes a man of God is able to keep himself under control at all times. He knows who he is in Christ Jesus and he knows the limits of his endurance. He knows the three times when he is most vulnerable to temptation: when he is hungry, when he is tired, and when he is running a low-grade fever. As a result, the man of God will want to get adequate sleep, regular and nutritious meals, and the right amount of exercise to keep his body in good condition. He will also keep a check on his mind so that his thoughts will not lead him astray. He does this by being careful about what he reads, watches, and listens to from the mass media. He knows that as a man thinks in his heart, so he will become in thought and deed (Proverbs 23:7).

The disciplined man knows how to handle his sexual tensions without undue distress. He knows that sexual pleasure was designed to be heterosexual within the bonds of marriage. He also knows that premarital sex is contrary to the Word of God and that adultery is a sin (Genesis 1:26-28; 2:18,21-25; Matthew 19:4-6; Hebrews 13:4; Ephesians 5;22; 1 Peter 3:1-7; 1 Corinthians 7:1-7). He knows that incest (sexual behavior between members of the immediate family) is against the law of God (Leviticus 18:6-17; 20:14; 1 Corinthians 5:1; 6:18). He further knows that homosexuality is the ultimate form of idolatry, worshiping the creature rather than the Creator (Leviticus 18:22; Romans 1:19-27), and that bestiality (sexual behavior with animals) is wrong (Exodus 22:19; Leviticus 18:23).

The disciplined male who is single or the married man who is apart from his wife because of vocational, military, or recreational reasons learns to sublimate his sexual feelings and convert them into constructive pursuits. Walt Menninger defines and illustrates sublimation in *Happiness Without Sex:*[3]

> A definition of "normal" sexual behavior is not easy to make. Extremes—excessive sex or complete abstinence —often signal emotional problems. A promiscuous woman may engage in excessive sexual activity to avoid emotional intimacy, despite a great deal of physical intimacy; and often her sexual activity fails to give her any real pleasure or satisfaction. Abstinence [within marriage] can likewise be a means to avoid intimacy, and it may also reflect underlying psychological problems.
>
> Yet there are occasions when one's needs for pleasure are adequately satisfied through nonsexual activities. This is achieved through a process which is labeled sublimation—the mental process by which basic sexual drives are unconsciously converted into other socially acceptable endeavors. One thereby achieves substantial

and lasting sources of satisfaction in life through work, play, [and] social and religious activity. In general, the greater one's capacity to sublimate, the better one's emotional health.

This process is evident in exceptionally mature people, whom Abraham Maslow has characterized as "self-actualizing." From his studies, Maslow concluded that "loving at a higher need level makes the lower needs and their frustrations and satisfactions less important, less central, more easily neglected.

Although Menninger is speaking from a psychological point of view, he is consistent with Biblical truth. The male adult, single or married, must develop a sensitive self-discipline that allows him to be a sexual person—masculine in every sense of the word—without feeling the compulsion to perform sexually. The single male sublimates his sexual energies, fully aware that they are normal, and saves himself for the bride of his choice. The married male separated from his wife exercises the same discipline which strengthens the marriage relationship that is based on mutual trust and fidelity. It is only in becoming a self-disciplined person that a man can become the kind of husband that God wants him to be.

Notes

1. Joyce Landorf, *Tough and Tender* (Old Tappan, NJ: Revell, 1975).
2. John Scanzoni, *Love and Negotiate* (Waco: Word Books, 1979).
3. Walt Menninger, *Happiness Without Sex* (Kansas City: Sheed, Andrews and McMeel, 1976).

Chapter 9
A Man As a Husband

A fellow and a girl who wed
Begin to live as one, 'tis said;
But many couples can't agree
Which one of them they wish to be![1]

In this chapter we will examine one of the roles of a marital relationship, that of the male half of the marriage: the husband. The role of husband is probably the most difficult task of being a Christian man. It is at this point that the expectations of a secular society collide with Biblical injunctions. When a man resolves these divergencies and integrates social and spiritual goals into being a consistent Christian and a faithful husband, he reaches the peak of his God-given potential as outlined in the initial chapters of Genesis. He is then man, created in the image of God, responding to God as a manager over the domain in which God has placed him.

WHAT IS A HUSBAND?

The word "husband" appears 120 times in Scripture. According to Webster, it comes from the Old English and means "master of a household" or "householder." The word is used to depict a married man as well as a frugal manager. When used as a verb, "husband" means "to manage prudently and economically." It is illustrated by the early Celt or Saxon man of England banding together shocks of grain to take home to provide for his household.

In the Old Testament the Hebrew word translated "husband" means "man" or "male person." In this setting the word has a root meaning of "master" and is used only in reference to laws concerning divorce and remarriage. The same word was later used to name the pagan god that Israel served when they rejected Jehovah and worshiped Baal. Throughout the Old Testament the word "husband" denotes maleness and masculinity in a marriage relationship.

In the New Testament the word translated "husband" also refers to man as male and masculine. The primary role of the husband in the Bible is that of a male person who has chosen to take to himself a wife and establish a marital relationship in the sight of God that is to last for a lifetime.

Fortunately, the adult male has the privilege of electing to remain single or else to marry and become a husband. Actually, marriage is a choice; it is not a requirement in life.[2] The man who is to enjoy marriage to the fullest will need to explore the gift of singleness to the full before he can really enjoy marriage.[3] Becoming the right person for a relationship is more important than finding the right person for a marriage partner.[4] To marry with the expectation of finding happiness in another person is an exercise in futility. The married male will be no happier than the single male unless he has prepared himself to be an adequate partner in a open relationship with the wife of his choice whom he receives as a gift from God at the marriage altar.

To be a husband in a Biblical sense is a many-faceted, complex role. It includes leadership, love, and commitment in addition to providing for the needs of a wife on many levels.

DIMENSION OF COMMUNICATION

It would be easy at this point to move into a discussion of the husband as the head of the house. But to be fair to the Biblical text, it is necessary to look at the entire fifth chapter of Ephesians in context to see the total relationship of husband and wife in marriage as God intended.

Paul begins his discussion with: "Be ye therefore followers of God, as dear children; and walk in love, as Christ also hath loved us, and hath given himself for us an offering and a sacrifice to God for a sweet-smelling savor" (Ephesians 5:1,2). He proceeds from verse 3 through the first half of verse 18 enumerating the things that Christians should not do. Then he makes a transitional declaration: "But be filled with the Spirit" (Ephesians 5:18). The following three verses show the importance of communication in three demensions of Spirit-filled living. Then the apostle examines the mutuality of responsiveness in marriage.

Communicate with Yourself

"Speaking to yourselves in psalms and hymns and spiritual songs, singing and making melody in your heart to the Lord" (Ephesians 5:19). Earlier we explored the importance of a healthy self-concept in becoming an adequate person. At that time we noted the importance of keeping a healthy, open communication with God in discovering who we are and why we are here so that we can determine through His will where we are going in life. It appears that Paul is referring back to the Great Commandment at this point to remind us that we must maintain a vital relationship with God and ourselves if we are to be adequate for the responsibilities of being a Christian husband.

This communication with self must be laced with praise and prayer. It should reflect our total submission to the will of God and express a desire to be led by His Spirit. This will be demonstrated in our thought life and spoken words. The openness of our relationship with God is enriched by the joy that comes by rehearsing phrases from the Psalms, contemporary hymns, songs, and choruses that magnify the Lord. Such self-communication encourages us to let His love flow through our lives as we reach out to those we love.

Communicate with God

"Giving thanks always for all things unto God and the Father in the name of our Lord Jesus Christ" (Ephesians 5:20). When we start each day with the awareness that God is our Father, it naturally follows that we will accept the unanticipated things of life as coming to us with His total awareness. Jesus taught against worry and anxiety (Matthew 6:25-34). He said that even a sparrow does not die without the knowledge of the Father (Matthew 10:29). Beyond that, Jesus Himself will not let the believer become embroiled in a situation beyond his control. The word "succor" in Hebrews 2:18 is from an old Anglo-Saxon root that means "jump and run to the assistance of." The Scripture literally says, "For in that he himself hath suffered being tempted, he is able to succor [jump and run to the assistance of] those who are being tempted."

Several years ago I conducted a family-enrichment conference for missionaries from nine Central American republics. We were in sessions morning, afternoon, and evening at a campsite outside Guatemala City. Thursday afternoon the women planned a shopping trip. Nita and I went into town with one of the missionary men who offered to be our guide and interpreter. I don't think I had ever seen my wife so happy as she browsed through the native market buying gifts for the family.

Returning to the campgrounds, we were driving on a one-way street. Out of nowhere a military vehicle loaded with soldiers struck our little Toyota and spun us around so we were headed the wrong direction. I looked into the back seat to see if Nita was all right. I was horrified to see her blood-spattered and unconscious. A huge knot was rising over the temple where her head had hit the rubber handle over the back door of the vehicle. My first thought was, "She's dead." I could not find a pulse.

Surveying the scene, the driver said, "I've killed your wife." At that moment I monitored my emotions to sense what I was feeling. I experienced a depth of peace that was so assuring that I said to my friend, "Don't worry. Nothing comes into the life of the believer without the presence of the Father. This is the time for us to ask Him, 'Lord, what are you wanting to teach us today?' "

I turned to the back seat, placed my hand on my wife's hand, and prayed a simple prayer, acknowledging God's presence and sovereignty and expressing my intense desire for healing for my wife. She opened her eyes, obviously in pain, but conscious and rational. Several hours of negotiations with the military authorities followed. We were treated with the utmost kindness and courtesy, with government medical facilities being made available to my wife. I declined, believing that the Lord would not have us be separated at that time. It was after dark when we returned to the conference grounds. After cleaning my wife up and putting her to bed, I watched as she slipped into a peaceful sleep and was by her side when she awakened the next morning—without a headache.

Did she ever have a shiner! She looked like the typical battered wife but was experiencing no discomfort. When we came through customs and immigrations in New Orleans a couple of days later I was the victim of dirty looks and stares from every official we passed. When we returned to Springfield and X-rays were taken, we were delighted to learn there was no evidence of a skull fracture. Only the discoloration of the eye confirmed what had happened. A spot of darkness collected under Nita's right eye. It is still there today, eight years later. Every time I look into my wife's eyes I see a gentle reminder that, but for the grace of God, I would have buried my wife in Guatemala. Instead, He has extended our time together. The dark spot under her eye is a gentle reminder several times a day of the value of "giving thanks always for all things unto God and the Father in the name of our Lord Jesus Christ." (Ephesians 5:20).

I sincerely believe that God does not inject circumstances

into our lives to make things difficult. Satan does enough of that and has done so since his initial encounter with Job (Job 2:1-7). But, what the devil or people may intend for evil, God will turn to good (Genesis 45:1-8). Christ is always with us and the Holy Spirit is available to guide us, even in the mundane affairs of life.

Communicate with Your Spouse

"Submitting yourselves to one another in the fear of God" (Ephesians 5:21). The implication here is mutual submission of the husband and wife to each other in the openness of communication that makes each one sensitive to the needs of the other. Since in Christ there is neither male nor female, bond nor free, the Christian husband and wife stand equal at the foot of the cross in their marital and family relationships (Galatians 3:28). It is the mutuality of concern and openness of relationships that makes it possible for the family to be truly Christian.

Paul's outline is simple: 1) wives submit (Ephesians 5:22); 2) husbands love (Ephesians 5:25,28,33); 3) children obey (Ephesians 6:1). In dealing with the relationship of the wife to her husband, Paul compares the headship of the husband in the home to the headship of Christ in the church. Although headship and love are interacting functions, we need to look at them separately in order to see how essential it is that they be exercised in balance.

EXERCISING HEADSHIP

When Paul declared that the husband should be the head of the wife, he gave an awesome command: "For the husband is the head of the wife, even as Christ is the head of the church; and he is the savior of the body (Ephesians 5:23). When the headship of the husband in the marriage is compared with the headship of Christ in the church, the text suggests that there are comparisons between what Christ did that Christian husbands should emulate. The basic question is:

what does a head do?

Since the human body is compared analogously with the body of Christ, the church, it may be helpful to look at what the head does as the depository of the brain in the central nervous system. Four principal functions come quickly to mind: 1) sensation, 2) perception, 3) cognition, 4) and communication.

Sensation

A head must be in touch with the sensory mechanisms of the body. Only as the eyes, ears, skin, nose, mouth, and other sensory receptors are functioning adequately and in touch with the central nervous system can they communicate the needs of the body. You hit your thumb with a hammer. A message is sent to the brain, "It hurts!" Until that message is sent, the rest of the body is oblivious to the pain that the thumb and hand are enduring. Through the God-given nervous system the message is carried to the head for processing: "My thumb hurts."

Perception

Perception is the process by which the brain takes the sensations coming from the body and puts them into perspective with memory and current awareness. When the pain in the thumb is perceived in relationship to the past, present, and possibly future welfare of the body, it is then possible for a course of action to be devised.

Cognition

A decision must be made because sensation and perception have placed the pain of the hand in proper relationship to the whole body. So a message is prepared to send back to the wounded hand to direct a proper response. This is where communication comes in.

Communication

The results of the decision made by the brain are communicated to the hurting thumb through the efferent nerves from the head to the hand. The message will no doubt be, "Move it." With this instruction, the hurting appendage is removed from the place where it could be hurt again. Other messages may well follow as to what to do to ease the pain.

Isn't that exactly how salvation began? God saw us in our sin, lost and hurting. He was sensitive to our need, perceived what we needed, and sent His Son to die for us. He communicated His plan to Christ, who in turn came to give His life for us (John 3:16,17). Jesus Christ initiated our salvation and made it possible for us to become children of God (Romans 8:14-17). And, as Head of the church, He continues to represent our needs before the Father (Hebrews 1:1-3; 7:25).

The root meaning of the word "head" is "enabler" or "one who makes it possible." As Christ is the *Enabler* of our salvation, the One who makes it possible for us to know God as Father and Himself as Lord, so the husband is to be the *enabler* of the wife, the one who makes it possible for her to respond to her husband with the same deference with which she submits to Christ as her Savior.

Note that the head of the human body does nothing for itself. The neural passages are connected to relay messages in and out of the brain, but there are no nerves designed to serve the brain itself, so it does not feel pain or function for its own benefit. Although this is only an analogy, it does reinforce the fact that the husband, as head of the wife, is not to be a dictator or potentate or to function in an authoritarian way with her. He is to be sensitive to her needs, put these needs in proper perspective, make decisions that will communicate his love for her, and act in such a way that his behavior will demonstrate the depth and intensity of his love for her.

SELFLESS LOVE

When the Christian husband sees himself in a true headship perspective, comparable to the way Christ initiated and consumated our salvation, he is then in a position to examine what it means to love as Jesus loved. The love of the husband for his wife is in the same category as the love of Christ for the church. The Greek word *agape* is used in each instance. Agape love is a selfless love, a love given with no thought of benefit returned. It is initiated by the lover and does not depend on the response of another person. So Paul could say, "Husbands, love your wives, even as Christ also loved the church and gave himself for it" (Ephesians 5:25). This implies that a man is to love his wife to the same degree that Christ loved the church. He gave His life for the church—His last ounce of energy, His last drop of blood. No better picture of selflessness could be portrayed than the words of this passage.

How can a man in human frame love his wife as much as Christ loved the church? Only by drawing on the same divine strength that took Christ through death, burial, and resurrection. It is neither convenient nor logical to demand this kind of response from a man toward a woman. Yet this is the kind of love that the Bible sets as the model for the Christian husband to follow in his marriage.

The implication: the husband is to love his wife no matter what she does, whether she deserves it or not. I once had a man come to a counseling session with the declaration: "I want a divorce." I asked him, "Why do you want a divorce?" He responded, "Because I don't love my wife anymore." I pointed him to this Scripture and said, "God commanded you to love your wife. It is a command, not an option. If you refuse to love your wife, you are in rebellion against God, and God's Word equates rebellion with witchcraft (1 Samuel 15:22,23). Let's deal with your sin, and then we can look at your marriage."

God never promised that a wife would be quiet, submissive, obedient, or passive all the time. A real man wouldn't want that anyway. The book of Hosea shows us that love can tolerate deliberate rejection and sin. But love can also restore and make whole (1 Peter 4:8). This is the kind of love that God wants in a Christian relationship—one that is selfless and forgiving.

Recognizing that the challenge of trying to love on the exalted level that Jesus loved might pose a problem, Paul elaborates on a more earthly level: "So ought men to love their wives as their own bodies. He that loveth his wife loveth himself. For no man ever yet hated his own flesh, but nourisheth and cherisheth it, even as the Lord the church" Ephesians 5:28,29). If you don't think you can love her on the exalted level of Christ's love, Paul is saying, love your wife at least as much as you love yourself. How much does a man love himself? He usually takes good care of himself. So love your wife and take as good care of her and her needs as you do your own. This is the kind of 50-50 relationship where you do for your wife equally as well as you do for yourself. This could imply that if you buy a new rifle or set of fishing tackle you would give your wife an equivalent amount in cash and ask no questions as to how she spent it. That could get expensive!

Simply, God does not want us to put limits on our love. The love of Christ is our model. We can look at how generous we are with ourselves in any dimension of life. This Scripture suggests that we should be just as generous with a wife as we are in meeting our own needs, both primary and secondary. When we are sensitive to the needs of our wife and see her needs in proper perspective from her point of view as well as our own, we can then make the kinds of decisions and initiate the kinds of behavior that will enhance our relationship. Our generosity with her will be a revelation of the depth of our love for her and for the Christ who has allowed us to share a relationship in which He is Lord.

COMMITMENT TO A RELATIONSHIP

When a man takes a wife to himself, he changes the nature of his relations with his own family. The new husband now becomes the head of a new family and must disengage himself from his family of origin. His primary energies must be devoted to the new relationship he has initiated. Paul quotes from both the Father and the Son when he says, "For this cause shall a man leave his father and mother, and shall be joined unto his wife, and they shall be one flesh" (Genesis 2:24; Matthew 19:5).

Commitment to a relationship in marriage is based on a man's commitment to God and to himself. When open communication exists between man and his Maker, he finds the strength to extend a commitment to the woman of his life. This commitment before God and society sets the new relationship apart as a viable entity in the community which involves fidelity to the marriage and refusing to allow outside pressures to impinge on the new unit.

Not only should the new couple move out on their own physically and geographically, but they must sever emotional ties that would make the family of origin more influential in their relationship than their new commitment to marriage. Too many times I have seen young people marry and move away, only for one of them to become homesick and rush back home to the parents, who received the returning person with open arms. Too frequently they compound the situation with subtle attacks on the estranged spouse that further alienate the relationship.

I shall never forget when Nita and I were prepared to leave our wedding reception for our honeymoon. Our plans were to leave that night for a job almost a thousand miles away from both of our parents. Her father held both of us by the hand and said to his daughter, "I love you, but don't ever come home without him." She never has, even though I'm sure she has been tempted to many times in the 32 years of our marriage!

The traditional words in the marriage vow are not idle prose: "For better or for worse, in sickness and in health, in poverty or in prosperity, until death shall separate us." It is only when a husband is committed to this ultimate separation from family and societal pressures that he can give unreservedly of himself to his wife in marriage as God planned.

PROVIDER

From the first day out of the Garden of Eden it has been the responsibility of a husband to provide for his wife and family:

And unto Adam he said, Because thou hast hearkened unto the voice of thy wife, and hast eaten of the tree of which I commanded thee, saying, Thou shalt not eat of it: cursed is the ground for thy sake; in sorrow shalt thou eat of it all the days of thy life; thorns also and thistles shall it bring forth to thee; and thou shalt eat the herb of the field; in the sweat of thy face shalt thou eat bread, till thou return unto the ground; for out of it wast thou taken: for dust thou art, and unto dust shalt thou return (Genesis 3:17-19).

The task of being a provider is the most constant demand of marriage. If a man sleeps eight hours a night and works eight hours a day, that leaves only eight hours for relationships. From the eight relational hours there has to be subtracted all the time spent in commuting to and from work plus fulfilling all other obligations to family, church, and society. The result is obvious: more time is spent in providing *for* the family than in being *with* the family. Therefore the job, vocation, or profession that a man chooses as the vehicle for providing for his family is extremely important.

The three most important choices a man will ever make in his life are these: 1) the choice of Christ as Lord, 2) the choice of a career, and 3) the choice of a companion. And these questions are best answered in this order. The man who chooses a companion before making the proper spiritual and vocational choice runs a big risk of introducing unnecessary conflicts into his marriage. The man who makes his career choice before his spiritual choice runs the risk of limiting himself to what he could have done if he had put Christ and His will first in his life. True, this will not interfere with his ultimate salvation, but it will set limits on the kinds of things he can do in his career because of lack of preparation or freedom of movement.

A wife has a right to know what career options are apt to affect the marriage relationship. That is why young people are advised to delay marriage until they have selected a career goal and then have initiated the educational and experience sequences essential for admissions into the field of their choice. Those who interrupt their education for marriage and then try to handle both marriage and school run into many unforeseen difficulties. It has been estimated that from two-thirds to three-fourths of the marriages launched in undergraduate education break up during graduate school or within two years after graduation.

In the third of a century I have taught, I have watched many young people start college. The track record for those who have completed their education and then married is far superior to those who married before or during their college years. Either the husband or wife had to drop out of school to put the other one through. In most cases when this has happened, neither has been able to go on as far as originally contemplated. Also, the one who dropped out harbored a nagging awareness in midlife that the sacrifice of a career may have been more disappointing than had been anticipated.

The young man who wants to be a good provider as a husband should seriously consider delaying the wedding until he has completed the education or apprenticeship necessary for admission into his career. Then he can devote his full energies to marriage without being distracted. Otherwise, something will have to give, for emotional energy is not sufficient to maintin a good marriage relationship while being distracted by studies and work.

Another caution in this regard is to avoid the temptation to become emotionally indebted to the family on either side by remaining on the family "dole" (allowing parents to pay tuition or support while you finish getting ready for your career). These gifts, as free as they may appear on the surface, have a strange way of concealing strings attached. Ultimately these strings have to be severed, sometimes abruptly and with pain. A gift as a gift may be helpful, but a young couple must be careful that there are no secret agendas or expectations that could later appear as bribes or manipulations that would hinder the young marriage.

The commandment to leave mother and father and cleave to the wife is both geographical and emotional. Live in your own place and establish your own way of life as a couple without neurotic bondage to the family of origin on either side. Working this out must be a part of the courting period, for it is too late to do it after the marriage has been consumated.

SEXUAL PARTNER

As a loving partner in marriage, a husband needs to be sensitive to the emotional and sexual needs of his wife as well as honest about his own needs. This is where the truth, the whole truth, and nothing but the truth is essential in a transparent relationship. I think this is what God meant in Genesis 2:25: "And they were both naked, the man and his wife, and were not ashamed." Rather than referring merely to physical nudity with emphasis on genital exposure, I believe this simply says that Adam and Eve had nothing to hide from each other. Theirs was an open, transparent relationship and it remained that way until Eve began to question God's word after listening to Satan in the serpent (Genesis 3:1-5).

Transparency in a marriage requires both husband and wife to be open and honest about feelings: hopes and fears, joys and sorrows. This takes communication beyond the cliche level of exchanging pleasantries and discussing the facts of a day's work to getting into feelings and honest disclosures of inmost thoughts. This is true intimacy and is achieved only when two people share a mutuality of trust and openness.[5]

It is in the expression of sexual love that transparent intimacy reaches its perfection. Paul refers to this shared sensitivity in 1 Corinthians 7:1-6. He basically says that no matter who initiates intercourse, husband or wife, each should respond totally and lovingly, rejecting the temptation to withhold sexual pleasure for any reason except a mutually shared spiritual burden. In that event, both should concentrate on prayer and fasting and then return to the marriage bed with the new excitement that comes from having resolved a spiritual crisis. This Scripture leads me to believe that Christians enjoy the expression of sexual love more than those who do not know God. For lovemaking between the Christian husband and wife is taking a gift from God and exploring its pleasures as a sacrament of thanksgiving for God's workmanship and is performed in His presence.

In the introduction to his book *Christian: Celebrate Your Sexuality* Dwight Small says:

Sexuality is an expression of the whole person; it belongs to the symphony of human existence. It cannot be compartmentalized, but is the music of the body, complete with rhythms and melodies and harmonies. Throughout the relationship of marriage there plays, as it were, the obligato of sexual love. . . .

Man is infinitely larger than the current theories of human sexuality take him to be. For if human sexuality is less than the mystery of human selfhood—including the mystery of man's relationship with God—then it is less than thoughtful men know it to be. The meaning of sexuality is the meaning of man himself.[6]

By hormonal nature and cultural training many men are more interested in reducing their own sexual tensions than in communicating love to their wife. That is why it is important for open communication to allow the husband and wife to discuss freely their needs and expectations in sexual activities. A man needs to realize that from the moment he enters the house after a day of work he is either preparing his wife for loving responses or building up barriers that will make love-making impossible. It is by touching and sharing in the kitchen, dining room, and family room that two hearts are prepared to unite their bodies in an act of love. But each must communicate to the other what nonverbal behaviors are desirable.

When Nita and I were first married I used to come home from school, look for her in the kitchen, and throw my arms around her. Usually she would be standing at the sink with her hands in the dishwater. She would get stiff as a board when I hugged her. I was perplexed. So I said, "I don't understand you. When dad did that, mother just melted into his arms." Her reply was curt: "I'm not your mother! Besides, I don't like to be bothered when my hands are wet."

The next night when I came home and headed into the kitchen, I picked up the first tea towel in sight and held it out as I approached her. She turned around, dried her hands, and responded in a spontaneously loving way. We had both learned a lesson. I was able to tell her what I wanted; she let me know that there was a better way to initiate affection. We had communicated and the result was pleasing to both of us.

It should also be noted at this point that depression lowers the sex drive and anger makes it impossible to enjoy the mutuality of sexual expression. Too frequently I hear the complaint in my office, "All he wants is sex." This is usually followed by "I feel like a piece of meat" or "I feel no better than a stick of wood." A number of writers have given some excellent psychological, spiritual, and physical suggestions to assist Christian husbands in initiating and expressing their love sexually.[7]

Erik Erikson presents a concept of genital utopia which, though secular in origin, is consistent with Biblical truth. He says:

In order to be of lasting social significance, the utopia of genitality should include:

1. mutuality of orgasm
2. with a loved partner
3. of the other sex
4. with whom one is able and willing to share a mutual trust
5. and with whom one is able and willing to regulate the cycles of
   a. work
   b. procreation
   c. recreation
6. so as to secure to the offspring, too, all the stages of a satisfactory development.[8]

In this chapter we have tried to look at the role of a man as a husband. It is a demanding role, one that should be initiated deliberately, spiritually, and intelligently, and one that must be cultivated constantly. For it opens the options for yet another role that many men choose to fulfill in life—the role of being a father.

Notes

1. Henry Brandt and Homer Dowdy, *Building the Christian Home* (Wheaton: Scripture Press).

2. Raymond T. Brock, *The Christ-centered Family* (Springfield, MO: Radiant Books, 1977).

3. Harry Hollis, Jr., *Thank God for Sex* (Nashville: Broadman Press, 1975).

4. Raymond T. Brock, *Dating and Waiting for Marriage* (Springfield, MO: Radiant Books, 1982).

5. H. Norman Wright, *Communication: Key to Your Marriage* (Glendale: Gospel Light Publications, 1974). *The Pillars of Marriage* (Glendale: Gospel Light, 1979).

6. Dwight H. Small, *Christian: Celebrate Your Sexuality* (Old Tappan, NJ: Fleming H. Revell Company, 1974).

7. Lewis B. Smedes, *Sex for Christians* (Grand Rapids: William B. Eerdmans), 1976. Ed and Gaye Wheat, *Intended for Pleasure* (Old Tappan, NJ: Fleming H. Revell, 1977). Dennis Guernsey, *Thoroughly Married* (Waco: Word Books, 1976).

8. Erik H. Erikson, "Eight Ages of Man," in Leon Gorlow and Walter Katkovsky, *Readings in the Psychology of Adjustment,* 2nd edition (New York: McGraw-Hill, 1968), p. 311.

Chapter 10
A Man As a Father

There is no higher calling for a man than to be a father. It is a demanding role but one that places him in a position of pointing his family to God and establishing the guidelines of family living. The man who has a consistent personal walk with God will find it easier to fulfill this role than one who tries to devise by human intellect the path in life into which young lives should be channeled.

It is evident that the confidence with which a man faces fatherhood will reflect how well he handles being a husband. Fortunate is the man whose marriage is childless for a sufficient number of years to allow the development of open communication in the relationship and the establishment of a confidence in the marriage that will make a secure home into which children can be invited. But when that magic hour arrives and a man experiences that enlargement of heart that propels a husband into fatherhood, he is faced with a new set of demands for which there is no adequate training.

PROVIDER

There are a variety of ways in which a father must be a provider for his family. He must certainly take into consideration the physical needs of the family and the emotional as well as the spiritual needs of the children. At the same time he must not neglect the needs of his wife. He must also remain loyal to himself and sustain his personal relationship with God.

Physical

The early chapters of Genesis chronicle the development of a variety of jobs that served as the basis for developing the first civilization. Adam was a farmer, and it was into this atmosphere that Cain, Abel, and Seth were born. Cain managed the farm while Abel handled the flocks until murder broke up the first family team. Apparently Seth took over the shepherding job after the death of Abel. Enoch, the first grandson of Adam and Eve, initiated construction and built a city, which he named for himself. A few generations later Jabal led his family off into a nomadic life of living in tents and tending cattle. His brother Jubal invented musical instruments, and Tubal-cain, a half brother, began to work in iron and brass and established the first trade school (Genesis 4).

Work productiveness goes all the way back to the first family. From the beginning, crafts and skills have been taught in the family and handed down from generation to generation. New crafts have been invented as the need arose, and the trend continues today. It is now estimated that half of the jobs that will be available to young people 20 years from now have not even been invented yet because of the increase of technology and the proliferation of knowledge.

In all of the busyness of plying his profession, a man must not neglect his family. As we noted earlier, a man must avoid the temptation to work for the sake of work and must refuse to isolate himself from his family. True generativity allows him to enjoy his work and be good at it, but at the same time he must not rob his family of its father.

Emotional

In a family counseling session recently, when a mother, father, and several children were present, the youngest observed, "I dread to see Daddy come home. I don't know if he's going to hit me or play with me."

Children need to experience unconditional love from their father, the same as all believers experience unconditional love from our heavenly Father. Meeting physical needs of children is not enough. They must have their emotional needs met and know they are a part of what is making the family function.

Since I did not complete my doctorate until I was 45, the study process was a family project. I shall never forget the feeling when I returned home the day I passed the orals over my dissertation and the degree was assured. When I opened the front door, the living room was draped with paper streamers and balloons, and a huge poster over the sofa read, "Welcome home, Dr. Daddy!" The shout of welcome that greeted me was, "We made it! We made it!" Yes, "we" made it because I could not have done it without the encouragement and support of my wife and three children, who allowed me the time and space necessary to complete the degree.

Nita and I have tried from the earliest of our family years to allow each child time and space to be a person. One of them in childhood (Joan) said to her mother, "I know you're trying hard to be a good mother, but you're a miserable failure. You're trying to love all of us alike, and I just need more love than the other two."

It is true that each child's emotional needs are different. The father needs to assess these individual differences and seek ways to communicate love and acceptance in the proportion demanded without becoming overprotective or solicitous.

Joan said to me on her 21st birthday, "You're trying too hard and loving us too much. You make too many of our decisions for us and overprotect us so that we won't be able to stand alone when we leave home and get our own jobs and apartments." I agreed with her that I in fact did love her too much, and I told her I was willing to try to change. I said, "I think you're right and I need you to help me to change. Let's make a deal. The next time you have something go wrong with your car, don't call me."

It was hardly two weeks before she had locked her keys in

her car. Honor would not allow her to call me, so she let her mother call me. I took care of the situation as usual, but we both agreed that it was a move in the right direction. Months later, when she had graduated from college and moved to another city to seek employment, she called me and said, "Dad, I have to make an adult decision and I need some help." Now she was able to call on me for advice when she wanted it and listen to my suggestions without my intervening in her adult life.

Spiritual

The father is first and foremost the priest of his household. It is his responsibility to set the spiritual tone of his family and bring his children up in the "nurture and admonition of the Lord" (Ephesians 6:4). The devotional life of the family is set by the father as he illustrates to the family the love and concern of God for His own children. This involves prayer at the appropriate times (mealtimes, family devotions, bedtime). It also involves the atmosphere of the home in which the father sets the example of self-discipline so that the children learn the controls that are appropriate to their age and stage of development.

Worship in the family is far more than reading the Bible and formal prayers, although these are important. True worship is both mother and father living before the children in such a way that they see Christ in the lives of their parents and build a desire to know the Lord that the parents serve. Such attitudes are "caught" as well as taught. The father's role in spiritual leadership is essential and God-given (Ephesians 5:23; 6:4; Colossians 3:21).

EXAMPLE

A father is on duty 24 hours a day. There is no time when he is off duty, because every moment that he is with any member of his family his example is being observed. It is at this point that it is most crucial for men to be men—to demonstrate in everyday life what Christian manhood is all about. The boys need it as an example to follow; the girls need it to know what manhood is so that they will have the right expectations when they begin to circulate in mixed groups and begin the processes of selecting a mate.

Values

What a man *is* speaks so loudly that his children do not always listen to what he says. Studies suggest that the kind of relationship which a girl has with her father between ages 12 and 16 pretty well set the expectations with which she will approach her relationships with males that will ultimately guide her in the choice of her own husband.

I made this observation in the missionary conference in Guatemala mentioned in the previous chapter. I went so far as to say, "If you don't like your son-in-law, gentlemen, go look in the mirror." Peals of laughter rocked the audience and everyone looked at a dignified, white-haired gentleman sitting between two attractive young ladies who were flanked by handsome young men. I was informed that these were the daughters of the older missionary. They had so admired their father and his consistent walk with God that their criteria for a husband had included the kinds of goals and values that were consistent with the demands of missionary involvement. Now that the senior missionaries have retired, both of the young couples have remained on the mission field with their own children.

Work Productiveness

The dignity of labor and the joy of hard work is best taught by example. Children of both sexes need to see their father helping in the kitchen and around the house as well as caring for the yard and car. Children who work with their parents learn skills that will be valuable to them when they are out on their own.

I was rather pleased last summer when our two older children (Cindy and Joan) chose to move from the family home and take jobs in Dallas. Cindy, an elementary education major with an emphasis in early childhood development, took a job as first-grade teacher in a Christian day school. Joan, the sociology major, took a job working with people in a helping relationship. They now have their own apartment and are exploring the dimensions of singleness.

In another year our son will graduate from college and make a similar move on his own. In the meantime he is involved with his mother and me in a ministry which includes marriage and family enrichment seminars, books, tapes, and a counseling service. He is learning the flexibility required to switch from being son in one setting to being business manager of a corporation in another. He is becoming expert at both tasks.

Stewardship

In the Christian family, stewardship must permeate the whole relationship. This involves the proper use of time and energy as well as resources. The father must set the example of fiscal responsibility in his financial offerings to the Lord but must also be judicious in the use of the remaining income so that its expenditure is pleasing to the Lord. He must distinguish between necessity and luxury, needs and wants, and he must set a standard for savings as well as insurance protection on both life and property.

How a man uses his time and energy will set the standard against which his children will measure the effectiveness of their own lives as they mature. They will either decide to follow their father as a model or else switch to an alternate lifestyle because they will have perceived his life as being unfulfilling or too demanding.

As a college counselor I have spent many hours with young people who were trying to hone out their future. I have seen them weigh parental example against its reward as viewed from the perspective of youth. I have seen many young men decide not to go into the family business or follow a father's trade because the net result was perceived as disappointing or not worth the effort. I have seen others sparked by the imagination of what more could be done by getting an earlier start in life. They have moved into a career choice that allowed for maximum expansion of skills with the attending satisfaction that comes from setting goals, implementing them, and reaping the results of hard work. Young people who are inspired get with the serious business of living life; those who are turned off have a way of becoming underachievers and settling for less than life could have offered them. The choice of direction begins in the home.

At this point it seems appropriate to remind fathers that children need room to make adequate decisions that will affect their future. Parents who make life too easy for their children do not allow them room to experience the results of choices, both good and bad. Children who do not get sufficient practice in decision-making develop what behavioral scientists call decidophobia, the fear of making choices. Freedom of choice must be followed with responsibility for the resulting behavior.

As each of our teenagers began to drive a family car, I told them I would assist them with insurance and upkeep but would not pay for any traffic violations or parking tickets. When this was tested, my wife and I held firm. As a result, one ticket is the maximum any one of them received!

TEACHER

To provide for the family and set the example of Christian living is not enough. Each father must become an expert teacher in the tasks of life that must be completed at each age of development. Children may see the overall scope of life, but they need individual instruction on how to handle the intricate details of specific life skills. Whether it is making a bed, picking up clothes and toys, setting the table, cleaning the garage, mowing the lawn, or washing the car, specific aspects of each task can be taught in such a way as to make work productiveness in the family more enjoyable and less time- and energy-consuming for the child. Teaching how to do a task is as important as assigning the task to be done.

Some fathers may delegate this responsibility to the mother of the children. However, it is more efficient for both parents to be involved in all the activities of the house, both inside and outside. Both boys and girls need to learn how to do a variety of things that they will need when they are out on their own in society. Our family calls these "survival skills." The value of teaching the skills is revealed when a boy keeps a neat room at home, in a college dormitory, or in his apartment. It also pays off when a girl keeps her car in good shape, checking the oil and transmission regularly.

Self-Expression Skills

Communication in the Christian family is taught by both example and instruction. The father, as the head of the house, must set the example by the way he expresses himself with his wife in front of the children. They can see the skills in action and evaluate for themselves the better ways of making wishes known and responding to the expectations of other people. Paul gives the key in Ephesians 4:15 when he talks about "speaking the truth in love" as part of the process toward maturity.

Norm Wright also offers some good suggestions.[1]

1. *Speak for yourself rather than for others.* It is so easy to speak in broad generalizations and forget to be specific about what you want or how you feel. "Other men wouldn't put up with what I have to put up with" can be a very threatening remark. In this situation, other men are not important. It would be much better to speak for yourself and say something like, "You know, I'm having trouble dealing with how I feel when I come home from a day of work and find the breakfast dishes still on the table." The seriousness of the problem must be weighed against whether the wife has been home all day watching TV or whether she has been out working as many hours as the husband has.

When we lived in Africa I developed a real aversion to cobwebs. I used to say to our African steward, "Samuel, see this lace on the lampshade? That is cobwebs, not lace. I want you to dust the lamp very carefully." His response would be, "Ah, master has such good eyes!" But I had to point them out to him regularly. When Nita and I came back to the United States and we were in our own apartment, I noticed a cobweb forming in the corner of the bedroom. I said to her, "Honey, see that cobweb in the corner? It reminds me of Africa." Her response to me was, "You're taller than I am." We communicated: we each spoke for ourselves. I developed the habit of knocking down cobwebs as I saw them rather than making their removal a point of contention.

2. *Document your observations.* Giving reasons for your assumptions can help clarify what you are trying to communicate. "I'm awfully tired tonight; the traffic was horrible," can give the family a hint of why you may not be up to par when you first arrive home from work. My family has learned that faculty committee meetings are the most frustrating thing in my academic schedule. Since I have a committee meeting each Thursday of the school year, they have learned that Thursday night is not my best night at home. My wife has gone so far as to make Thursday night the best meal of the week. I noticed as the children were growing up that their demands were less on Thursday nights once they understood my frustrations.

3. *State how you feel.* Aroused emotions result from the way we perceive life. In the last chapter we noted that sensation precedes perception. If it is perceived as comforting, another response is appropriate. Since perceptions belong to us alone until they are shared, it is essential for the father to communicate to the family what he is experiencing and why he is responding the way he is. "It makes me very happy when you do such a good job of cleaning out the garage" can motivate a child to cooperative work. "It really makes me sad when I see you goofing off and letting your math grade

slip. I think you're capable of doing better and I believe you could make better use of your time if you really tried." Such an honest sharing between father and son just might make the difference between the child's being a pupil who slides along and a student who takes his education and future seriously.

4. *State what you intend to do.* When you have expressed yourself and given reasons for your position and the resulting emotional overtones, it is appropriate for the family to know what your intentions are. "Now that you have finished your homework, we can go out and play catch" can be a kind of rewarding statement that encourages the completion of a task. "You can't go to the park to play until you have finished cleaning your room" outlines the sequence of behavior expected from a child and permits him to plan accordingly. With the teenager it is the same: "Since it seems that you haven't learned to tell time yet and came home an hour late, I'll have to keep the car keys until Friday and give you time to decide if you're willing to abide by the curfew for weeknights."

Listening Skills

Listening skills are as important as self-expression skills. They are best taught by example followed with explanations as necessary.

1. *Concentrate on listening.* Listening is hard work. Those of us in the helping professions who spend a great deal of time listening will attest to the fact that listening is extremely exhausting. It is no easier at home than in the counseling office. It requires demonstrating interest and alertness to your wife and children, looking at them when they talk, and giving them undivided attention until they have finished. It also requires you to search for common meanings to the words being used in order to avoid misunderstandings. I'm still not sure when my son asks for "bread" if he's hungry or broke!

2. *Avoid interrupting.* Waiting until a child has completed saying what is on his mind can try your patience. It also

demands that you withhold evaluation until you understand the total message. One day Joan was asking for permission when I interrupted with a premature "No!" She looked me straight in the eye and said, "That's not fair. You interrupted before I was finished." I apologized, listened until she had finished, and discovered that I had made a snap decision on too little information. So I gave her the permission—not because of an argument, because there was none, but because I realized my error in judgment.

3. *Provide clear and immediate feedback.* Precision in communication at this point is crucial. You will have to repress the tendency to respond emotionally on many occasions. A response such as "You did *what*?" may very well stem the flow of information that is vital for effective family communication. You have a right to ask questions for clarification, but they need to be for information rather than condemnation. It is often helpful to rephrase what you think you heard to see if your interpretation is correct. Then you can proceed with your response according to your evaluation of the situation.

Discipline

Discipline is the introduction of control into the life of a child. It emphasizes *learning appropriate behavior* rather than threatening punishment as retribution for wrongdoing.

1. *How Christian fathers discipline.* The Christian father, as head of his household, should take the lead in the discipline of the children. He has three basic methods: a) modeling example, b) teaching, and c) reinforcing behavior. The father must demonstrate the skills of self-discipline as an example for his children to follow. He cannot get by with the cliche, "Do as I say, don't do as I do."

The teaching dimension of discipline involves clearly communicating what kinds of behaviors are appropriate and those which are off-limits. Then the father should give positive reinforcement for behaviors that are approved and withhold privileges when behavior is not appropriate. This three-pronged approach to discipline in the Christian home—example, teaching, and reinforcement—establishes the atmosphere in which self-discipline can develop.

2. *Guidelines for living.* Every home must have guidelines to establish what we called "latitude for liberty" in our home. Rules must be reasonable and within the ability of the child to perform. They should be clearly communicated in the language of the child. As the child matures and demonstrates that he can handle more freedom, the rules need to be redefined and expanded. Then, the rules must be consistently and lovingly enforced. It is only as rules are established and consistently enforced that they provide the structured security that a loving home establishes.

When I was 16 my father gave me the keys to the family car with the instructions: "Be home by ten." One night a couple of years later, when I was out with the girl to whom I am now married, I lost track of time. Too late I realized that I could not possibly get her home and make my own curfew (which was earlier than hers). So it was ten after ten when I walked in the front door.

Dad stood to his full six feet and stuck out his hand. He didn't say a word. I dropped the car keys into his hand, kissed him and mother goodnight, and went to bed. To this day he has not asked me why I was late and I have not bothered to tell him. Why? There was nothing to discuss. I was late: we both knew it, so there was no need for arguing.

The following Friday mother said to me, "Your keys are out on the mantel in the living room." I never lost the car keys again. I discovered, in the quiet, gentle way my father taught me, that rules were to be enforced consistently without anger. I also learned that if I needed to be out later than curfew, an explanation before leaving for the evening brought permission for an exception to the rule when the situation warranted it.

3. *Scriptural guidelines.* Second Timothy 3:16,17 gives four guidelines to assist Christian fathers in establishing a

code of discipline: "All Scripture is given by inspiration of God, and is profitable for doctrine, for reproof, for correction, for instruction in righteousness, that the man of God may be perfect, thoroughly furnished unto all good works."

"Doctrine" suggests that fathers need to use God's Word in giving their children a faith to live by. This will involve both example and teaching. "Reproof" refers to preventive interventions into behaviors that could become a problem; it includes both advice and counsel. "Correction" denotes both discipline and chastisement (Hebrews 12:6,7). "Instruction in righteousness" emphasizes teaching children better ways to handle old problems, defining the finer points of consistent Christian living.

4. *Using the "rod" in discipline.* Much misunderstanding has arisen about the use of the "rod" in discipline. The Hebrew word used by both David and Solomon has three basic meanings. The rod was first and foremost a *scepter of authority* in the family of David's time. It is pictured in the hands of the oldest member of a clan as the elders were grouped in council. Whatever decision they reached was enforced by the chief with the understanding that "the buck stops here" (cf. Psalm 23:4).

A secondary meaning of the word "rod" is that of a *counting stick.* This usage is illustrated by the shepherd using the rod to guide the sheep into the sheepfold at night. It was also the same instrument he used to nudge them away from the precipice to keep them from dropping over the cliff and away from the rapidly moving waters that would soak the heavy coat of wool and drag them to their death in the stream (cf. Proverbs 13:24; 29:15). The rod in the Christian family is an instrument of accountability to help children become responsible for their own behavior.

One of our girls was out with a group of friends. It was approaching the curfew hour when the phone rang. "It's five till 11," she said, "and I know you will hit the panic button at 11. So I thought I would call and tell you where I am." She went on to explain where the group was and asked for an extension of the curfew. I gave permission. Why? Because I believe that trust breeds trust. Joan had been consistently building up my confidence in her word so I had no reason to doubt her on this occasion. I was gratified later when I found out that the concert had lasted longer than expected and she was a guest of the performing group in an after-concert celebration.

The third meaning of the word "rod" is as a *weapon*. But the weapon was designed for use on the lion and bear, not the sheep. When Solomon talks about using the rod on the son, it is in a setting where the son has identified with the forces of evil, the lion and bear. The rod is an instrument of corporal punishment only to save the rebellious child from more serious evil (Proverbs 10:13; 23:13,14).

The use of the rod in a modern Christian family requires the father to set the example of Christian living and to establish Scriptural guidelines for family interaction. He will freely communicate his expectations with his children, will show their relevance to Scriptural teachings, and will give reasons why he has established such expectations. When rules are broken, the child must be held accountable for his behavior and must have privileges curtailed until appropriate behavior is restored. It is only when the child has rejected Biblical and parental guidelines and aligned with the forces of evil that more stringent interventions are appropriate, not to punish the child but to get his attention and direct him back to the paths of righteousness.

In passing, it is appropriate to note that the instruction "Train up a child in the way he should go, and when he is old, he will not depart from it" (Proverbs 22:6) literally means "teach the child how to suck and take the nourishment that is necessary to survive." Training is the beginning of discipline and continues throughout life as children are guided into a lifestyle that reflects the holiness and righteousness of a loving heavenly Father.

Attitudes and Values

Teaching of attitudes and values is a never-ending task. The father who has followed the principles of communication and discipline suggested in this chapter will have gone a long way in communicating to his family the attitudes that will guide their lives long afer they have left the parental home.

As we noted earlier, an attitude is a predisposition to respond consistently to the opportunities of life—people, places, ideas, concepts, etc. It incorporates the interaction of the total human personality—thinking, feeling, and responding. Attitudes begin with opinions and beliefs that weave together to form habits of thinking that predispose a person to respond spontaneously and consistently.

Attitudes are the foundation of values. Rokeach says that a value is "a type of belief, centrally located within one's total belief system, about how one ought or ought not to behave, or about some end-state of existence."[2] In a comparative summary he says, "An adult probably has tens or hundreds of thousands of beliefs, thousands of attitudes, but only dozens of values. A value system is a hierarchical organization—a rank ordering—of ideals or values in terms of importance."[3]

The teaching of attitudes and values is the most important function of fathering. It gives children guidelines for living and it gives youth examples to follow. The father's message to his family should be, "Follow me as I follow Christ" (1 Corinthians 11:1).

There is really only one thing a father can take from this life into eternity with him: his family. Fortunate is the father who so lives before his children that they will choose to follow his footsteps into eternity and gather as a unit around the eternal throne!

Notes

1. H. Norman Wright, *Communication and Conflict Resolution in Marriage* (Elgin, IL: David C. Cook Publishing Co., 1977), pp. 4-5.
2. Milton Rokeach, *Beliefs Attitudes and Values* (San Francisco: Jossey-Bass Inc., Publishers, 1970), p. 124.
3. Ibid.

Chapter 11
A Man and His Work

It begins very early. At age two they're already saying, "Wow, he's grown so much! He's going to be a brute just like his father." Then at age six he picks up his first baseball bat at Little League when all the parents are around. They cheer as he hits a dribbler down the third base line and arrives safe on first. Then on the next play he's thrown out at second, and there is dead silence coupled with a few "That's okay, son" comments which are meant to console. Or are they? He can hear the difference between the prior enthusiastic cheers and the low-key consolations. Those big people want him to win. And he knows it.

All this gets reinforced even more as he enters scouting. He can see the awards, medals, and merit badges at each pack meeting. He looks down at his own vacant shirt and realizes that he'll have to get rolling in order to earn something to pin or sew on his uniform. Besides, several of his friends in Den 7 are already ahead of him. Daniel has earned his Wolf Badge. Steven just received his Bobcat.

Then at home that night during prayer time, Dad prays that Jimmy will work a little harder on his achievements so he too can receive the Wolf by the next pack meeting. Jimmy's got the message. Dad will be pleased if he does well, if he achieves.

Jimmy finds the same messages coming through at school among his peers. By age seven the boys are bragging, "Our soccer team hasn't lost a game; we're in first place," or, "My dad's bigger than your dad," or, "He makes more money than your dad." Or maybe it's more subtle, when he sees a good friend slipping away from him because the friend is more often chosen by the popular boys for a football game. Jimmy just doesn't quite have Daniel's skill at catching and throwing the ball.

But he must succeed at something. So perhaps Jimmy throws himself into his studies and is recognized for that. He may retreat from friendships and be labeled as an intellectual, but it's better than nothing. On report card day he knows he reigns superior over Daniel and most of the rest of the boys.

As he grows older, other boys are seen less as friends and more as competitors, potential threats to his own success pursuits. Therefore he begins to become more guarded around them, hiding his weaknesses, inadequacies, and vulnerabilities.[1] When adulthood arrives, a man has little choice but to compete. If he shows any inadequacies or discusses weaknesses with another man, he is likely to be shunned, or at least he believes he will be. I can remember going to pastors' meetings and hearing basically a bunch of bragging. "We have just started a new youth program that is bringing in young people like flies," or, "Our marriage enrichment weekend was just fabulous! We must have saved at least five marriages!"

Now you might be thinking, "Isn't there some reality to competition? Are we supposed to teach our boys never to compete? Won't they just get ground up in the process?" The answer is that we need to provide a balance. In other chapters we have discussed the burden of competitiveness and achievement placed on males. And of course as a man I know I live in a competitive world. I know that money is important in the sense that bills must be paid. Food, clothing, and shelter are family needs. I also know that our competitive world causes many people to behave like lions in a gladiator's arena.

For example, when I'm searching for a TV repairman I don't take the first fancy ad out of the newspaper and call that number. I check with friends and neighbors what their experience has been with TV repair people, and then I make my choice. I know I live in a world of fierce competition and manipulation to get money. So I don't lie down passively and merely allow the world to gobble up my family and me. But where is the balance?

THE WORK TRAP

By age 35 or so a man may be living in a nice home. He may have a couple of cars that he's making payments on. He's even managed to invest some of his hard-earned dollars in a money market fund, treasury bills, silver coins, or real estate. You'd think the man would now feel secure. In fact, he feels worse. You see, he has now moved to a more elite community, and the peer pressure is even heavier. Everyone in the neighborhood is going on trips to Mazatlan or Hawaii or Phoenix. And his kids must now wear Adidas shoes instead of department store shoes. So he must make even riskier investments. He really needs to work harder, because the thought of losing what he has and going backward is terrifying.

He begins to cheat in little ways on his income tax. Nothing big. After all, the government has all this graft going on and he has a right to even the score. Or perhaps the man steps on others a bit to get ahead. Maybe a few shady deals are approved in order to pull in enough bucks for that Audi 5000 or trip to Honolulu.

Where is all this going to end? Is there any perspective to all this—any truth?

ABOVE REPROACH

Earlier we discussed a Biblical perspective on maleness based upon 1 Timothy 3 and Titus 1. One of the first characteristics described by Paul in 1 Timothy 3:1-7 was that a Christian man should strive for being above reproach or of blameless reputation. As we stated before, to be above censure, above any reprimand or dishonor is quite a challenge. This means living as clean and moral a life as possible. How do we apply this principle to our work lives?

How often have you heard non-Christians say something like this? "It makes no difference whether a man is a Christian or not. He will still indulge in the same shady dealings as a nonbeliever. He pushes for an affair with his secretary. He leaves his debts unpaid, even those owed to Christian friends. In fact, I have had worse business dealings and have been ripped off more with Christians than with nonbelievers!"

When Paul came to Lystra on his second missionary journey he heard about Timothy. "He was well spoken of by the brethren at Lystra and Iconium" (Acts 16:2 RSV). He had a good reputation in two separate locations. He was living a Christian life, not only at home, but in another town as well. Not only was Timothy a model of decent living where people knew him and where the risks of being found out were greater, but he was also exemplary on the road, where he might get away with some questionable behavior.

Gene Getz in his book *The Measure of a Man* asked a group of men to list the words they would use to describe a man with a good reputation. I have made the same request as I've presented workshops for men. The lists are usually very similar. Here are some of the men's descriptions of a man with a good reputation:

He's trustworthy.

I'd want him to handle our estate if I died.

He's fair.

He's honest.

He doesn't let you down.

He will not take advantage of people.

I'd trust him with my bank account.

He is not an opportunist.

He admits his mistakes.

He's a hard worker.

I can count on him.

I could trust him to hold something in confidence..
I trust his judgment.
He is unassuming, humble.
He is not conceited.
He doesn't have to brag.
I can recommend him for any task.
He keeps his word.
He seems to care about people.
He asks about me.
He knows where he's going; he plans ahead.
He recognizes and respects authority.
He listens to me and respects me.

Without laying a guilt trip on you, how do you come out in some of these areas? You might retort, "Here you've told me that trying to achieve is bad. Now you're asking me to jump one more hoop by measuring up to man above reproach!" Wait a minute! I didn't say achievement is bad. I'm only suggesting that as men we tend to put all our eggs in the basket of worldly success and tend to forget about godly success. As we discussed earlier, we are secure and worthwhile because God chose us and sent His Son to die for us. We are significant and have a purpose when we strive for "godly success." And striving for a good reputation is moving toward godly success.

So now back to the question: at work, how "above reproach" are you? Do you engage in business practices that are questionable morally? Do you curse, tell dirty jokes, etc., just because you think it will keep you in the mainstream? How honest and fair are you with your colleagues? With your employees? Do you recognize and respect authority? Do you behave toward people in loving ways? What would a group of co-workers say about you when you're not present? Do you keep your word? Are you thoughtful, cordial, caring? Your answers to these questions will ultimately be more important than how much money you make, what neighborhood you live in, or whether your son starts on the football team. Sure, money is important. Your home and its atmosphere are important. Your son's success and achievements are important. But where does true significance come from—worldly success or godly success?

FREE FROM THE LOVE OF MONEY

Last year I wanted to make a fast buck. The Denver over-the-counter stock market was booming. I got into several new issues that paid off very well. Then I got the fever; and I became greedy. Frantically I checked the paper every day. I had a list of stockbrokers a mile long. All my thoughts, conversations, and spare time began to revolve around the stock market and how to get rich quick. I became consumed with greed. Then one of my stocks dropped. Then another. Now what? Sell? Buy more? Take a loss for a tax write-off?

I began to make some decisions based solely on emotions, and I dropped some money overnight. And I learned a lesson. The lesson is stated very clearly by Paul in 1 Timothy 6:9,10:

> People who want to get rich fall into temptation and a trap and into many foolish and harmful desires that plunge men into ruin and destruction. For the love of money is the root of all kinds of evil. Some people, eager for money, have wandered from the faith and pierced themselves with many griefs (NIV).

I had become so obsessed during that time that I neglected my work, my friendships, and my family. I had no time for God either. I was just too busy making money.

Money in itself is not evil. The Bible does not say a Christian should be "free from money" but rather "free from the love of money."[2] It is a matter or priorities. Jesus said, "But seek first his kingdom and his righteousness, and all these things [food and clothes] will be given to you as well" (Matthew 6:33 NIV). A man who loves money lays up "treasures upon earth" rather than "treasures in heaven" (Matthew

6:19,20). And as Jesus says, "Where your treasure is, there will your heart be also" (Matthew 6:21).

What does all this say about a man and his work? I believe it is saying that if we seek God's will first, He will bless us with what we need and what we can handle. I believe it is also saying that when we become nearsighted and make money our goal for security and significance, we're on shaky ground.

THE LAZY CHRISTIAN

The Bible is a marvelous book of balances. The Scriptures also have something to say about the Christian who takes advantage of other people monetarily. Paul wrote:

> If anyone will not work, neither let him eat. For we hear that some among you are leading an undisciplined life, doing no work at all, but acting like busybodies. Now such persons we command and exhort in the Lord Jesus Christ to work in quiet fashion and eat their own bread (2 Thessalonians 3:10-12 NASB).

Some people believe it is fashionable to be a Christian in poverty. They justify their laziness on the basis of "not loving money." I sometimes see evidence of this at the grocery checkout. In front of me is a young, strong man buying food, film, etc. with food stamps! I'm afraid that my thoughts are not "above reproach" at that moment. If this young guy is capable of work and is spending someone else's income tax money, I don't believe it's what the Lord had in mind. Man is, by command from God, to earn his living by the "sweat of his face" (Genesis 3:17-19).

Again, some questions. Are you obtaining money in deceitful or dishonest ways? Are you giving some money away for worthy causes? Do you use some of your money to care for other Christians who are in need? Or are you living off other people in a lazy and irresponsible way?

BE A SERVANT

Have you ever noticed how one person seems to treat his job and you in a warm, considerate way? I have been served by waiters who were warm and kind and also by waiters who were cold and inconsiderate. I have known competent mechanics who were "servants" and also those who were sociopaths intent on manipulation and greed. I have been to physicians who ministered to my physical and emotional needs, and I have also been treated by doctors whose only interest was in their own personal gains. Matthew 20:26,27 states, "Whosoever will be great among you, let him be your minister; and whosoever will be chief among you, let him be your servant." Loosely translated, this means, "Whoever will be great among you, let him minister unto the people's needs; and whoever will be chief among you, let him give service in that field in which he is most skilled."

OVERCOMMITMENT

We need to always remember two simple points about life: *life is short* and *death is certain*. Some years ago we received a plaque that said:

> Only one life,
> 'Twill soon be past;
> Only what's done
> For Christ will last.

At the time I thought, "How terribly trite!" But as each year ticks off I realize more deeply the basic truth in that statement.

When we are overcommitted to anything that takes us away from meaningful relationships we need to come back to these truths. *Life is short. Death is certain.* Only what's done for Christ will last. It's amazing how simple truths can be extremely profound.

Are you so committed to your work that your family members never get on your "to do" list? "Some day, honey,

we will." "If you'll just wait until I'm done with this report."
"I just took on a new position at work and I have several
projects that must be completed by the end of the year. Every
Saturday and most evenings have to be devoted to that. My
son keeps asking me to fly a kite with him and go fishing and
stuff, and I wish I could. I keep telling him that if he can wait
until next summer we'll have a lot of time to do those
things."

The scariest part of all this is that we often see overcommit-
ment as a temporary problem. But there is "temporary"
problem after "temporary" problem until temporary
becomes chronic, and we end up never having ministered
adequately to our family.

Notes

1. Herb Goldberg, *The Hazards of Being Male* (New York:
   New American Library, 1977).
2. Gene Getz, *The Measure of a Man* (Glendale: Regal
   Books, 1979).

Chapter 12
The Myth of Being an Old Man

Jeremy was old before his time. Throughout his years he had taken life too seriously. He had never taken time to play, relax, or enjoy living at any age. He looked only to the future, letting his youth slip by in his eagerness to "grow up" and then to "live." Unfortunately, he did not develop the coping skills necessary to face new challenges in his life, and he "burned out" at an early age.

By 35 he was a business success. His family was well on their way to affluence. But financial reversals and conflicts with his corporate partners were beyond his ability to handle them. As a result, he took to his bed. Convinced he was sick, Jeremy sank into a state of semihelplessness. He required constant care from his family. As his condition deteriorated, they put him in the nursing home where I was administrator. When I first met Jeremy, he was barely 60 and a bed patient.

I became distressed that Jeremy's family showed little concern for their father and seldom visited him. So I called a family conference. It was then that I learned that "age" was a game that Jeremy had learned to play and that helplessness was a maneuver to control his family. When they did not respond to his beck and call, he would become more helpless in order to manipulate them. What he had not expected, however, was that helplessness brings muscle atrophy. A decade of such withdrawing behavior had left Jeremy physically weak and emotionally depleted. Now he was actually infirmed, but not as sick as he had led himself to believe.

After the family conference and consultation with the doctor, I went to Jeremy and informed him that we could no longer provide a nurse to feed him in bed. I placed a walker in his room and told him he would have to get himself to the dining room if he wanted to have regular meal service. After much protest—with tears—Jeremy slowly got out of bed, took small steps across the room, and inched his way down the hall to the dining room. An aide helped him to a table. For the first time in months, Jeremy sat at a table eating and socializing. At first he only listened to conversation, but before long he joined in to make his contributions. He was now being his age. A year later, when I resigned from the hospital staff, Jeremy was still alert and ambulatory, although weakened and slowed by his years of inactivity. He had become too old too soon and had lost the support of his family in the process.

Josh, on the other hand, was just the opposite. He enjoyed his youth and carried it creatively into his mature years. He had still been teaching college at 70 and could swing such a mean tennis racket that he held his own against any student on campus. He and another professor, now both nearing 80 and retired, teamed up for doubles and won the tennis competition at the annual student-faculty meet.

He was already past retirement age when he came into his theology class one morning and opened the session by singing the Burgermeister Beer commercial, much to the consternation of his seminary students. Then he said, "I heard that on the radio while I was shaving this morning and I can't get it off my mind, so there it is. Now let's get on with the lesson." Then he opened his Bible and began to expound on the finer points of theology.

When Josh was 90 he lost his wife. I helped him up the half-flight of stairs to the viewing room to see her for the first time in her coffin. He wept appropriately, shared some endearing memories with her, patted her hand, and moved to an easy chair to receive friends who had come to share their consolances. At age 92 he fell and broke his hip but was ambulatory again in a remarkably short time. Although Josh is physically feeble, he just doesn't know how to get old in spirit. He is eternally young.

CULTIVATING AGELESS ATTITUDES

Age is a state of mind. A man may be old while the calendar says he should be young, or he may remain young while his body ages. In Solomon's words, "For as he thinketh in his heart, so is he" (Proverbs 23:7). Being an old man is a myth to those who develop an attitude toward aging that is ageless. If a man thinks he is getting old, he will convince himself to act old. If he believes he is still capable of constructive, creative living, he will keep young at heart and think creatively even though his physical powers decrease and his mobility is slowed by the normal processes of aging.

Paul gave us the way to achieve ageless attitudes when he said:

> Your attitude should be the kind that was shown us by Jesus Christ, who, though he was God, did not demand and cling to his rights as God, but laid aside his mighty power and glory, taking the disguise of a slave and becoming like men. And he humbled himself even further, going so far as actually to die a criminal's death on a cross (Philippians 2:5-8 TLB).

If we will learn to think as Jesus thought, by developing His attitudes toward the challenges of life, we can live as He wants us to live in the present generation. The attitudes of Christ, outlined in the Beatitudes (Matthew 5:3-12), give men of all ages appropriate ways to look at life and ideas of how to respond to its challenges.

The positive lifestyle that comes from a personal relationship with Christ gives the maturing man an outlook on life that frees him for creative living. Paul encourages, "Fix your thoughts on what is true and good and right. Think about things that are pure and lovely, and dwell on the fine, good things in others. Think about all you can praise God for and be glad about" (Philippians 4:8 TLB). This will result in bearing the fruit of the Spirit in daily life: "But when the Holy Spirit controls our lives he will produce this kind of fruit in us: love, joy, peace, patience, kindness, goodness, faithfulness, gentleness and self-control; and here there is no conflict with Jewish laws" (Galatians 5:22,23 TLB).

MEASURING AGE

Aging begins with birth. Each stage of development brings with it a new set of challenges and requires adjustment to the changes of life. The male has to learn to be a child, then a youth, and ultimately an adult if he is to explore the dimensions of masculinity. Within adulthood he has to learn to be a young adult, a middle-aged adult, and then an older adult. There are basically three kinds of aging that a man must experience: biological, psychological, and social.

Biological Aging

Biological aging relates to the changes in the organism's vulnerability. Studies indicate that as men pass age 50 their sensitivity to pain declines, but the rate of decline varies in different parts of the body. Brain size begins to decrease after 30, but intelligence remains constant for a much longer time, usually not decreasing appreciably until within five years of death. Ironically, the need for sleep decreases with age, so that when a man has time for sleep his system demands less of it. "Catnaps" appear to be more a function of boredom than of physiological necessity.

Middle age brings an increase in heart attacks for men, with four out of five heart attacks reported for the middle-aged being experienced in the male segment of the population. Birren has noted that "masculinity, high activity or drive, productivity, and responsibility appear positively related to the development of cardiac disease."[1] It is also noted that the older the man, the longer it takes for his heart to recover from strenuous exercise.

Hormonal changes in the male organism bring about midlife changes called the climacterium. Compared to the menopause in women, climacterium in the male has less physiological involvement and appears to be less abrupt and to extend over a longer period of time. Fertility in the male can last into the advanced years of the seventies and eighties, however. Charlie Chaplin was past 80 when he fathered his last child by Oona O'Neill, and this phenomenon is reported common among Indian men of the Peruvian Andes and the Azerbaidzhan Republic of the Soviet Union.

Aging brings less sensitivity of the taste buds, but men seem to be subject to more digestive diseases than women. The efficiency of smell decreases with age, as does visual acuity, leading to presbyopia (old sight) or farsightedness. Brighter illumination is required for reading and other visual activities. The ability to hear high-pitched sounds begins to decrease after 40; hearing loss is greater for men than for women in the adult years. This may result from more exposure to noise because of their occupational settings, particularly in industrial societies, where men are subjected to higher decibel levels (jackhammers, airplane engines, factory machinery, etc.).

Unfortunately, studies confirm what men have feared: American men show the signs of aging at an earlier age than do women. Breathing becomes more labored after age 40 because of a decline in the basal metabolic rate. The voice of the male becomes more high-pitched as he progresses from middle age to old age.

Very few changes are noted in the central nervous system of the aging male until late into senility. However, the older the male the less efficient his short-term memory. But older men show the ability to solve the everyday problems of life equally as well as do younger men.

Vincent has observed, "Until we are 35 or 40, our faces are those that God gave us; after that they are the faces which we make for ourselves."[2] Bischof notes that "it would seem apparent, then, that a dissolute past will be written upon the faces of those who indulge themselves in wasteful pursuits" and recalls Abraham Lincoln's oft-quoted comment, "After

40 a man is responsible for his own face."[3]

Responding to the age-old question "Can an old dog learn new tricks?" Bischof says concerning the aging male:

> And so we come to the general conclusion that the old dog can learn new tricks, but the answer is not a direct and simple one. It appears that the old dog is reluctant to learn new tricks. He is less likely to gamble on the results, particularly when he is not convinced that the new trick is any better than the old tricks, which served him so well in the past, but learn it he does. Further, the best evidence seems to indicate that if he starts out as a clever young pup, he is very likely to end up a wise old hound.[4]

Psychological Aging

How a man perceives what is happening to him physically as he experiences the aging process will have a profound influence on his psychological vitality. There is no evidence to suggest that emotional breakdowns or psychological problems are more prevalent in middle age than in the younger years. However, it is evident that the coping mechanisms developed in youth will determine to a significant degree how the aging man deals with life. When breakdowns do occur in the adult years it appears that they come as a result of a history of unresolved problems associated with a lack of direction in life, a lack of self-understanding, and a lack of purpose or goals in life.[5]

Horney believes that the pressures of an industrialized society and the inability of a man to get along with his fellowmen appear to be primary factors leading to emotional breakdowns.[6] Billig has noted that "middle-aged conflicts for lower- and middle-class men were based primarily upon family, relations with younger business associates, and attempts to prove sexual abilities by extramarital affairs."[7] The man who has not resolved his emotional conflicts in adolescence and his young adult years may find that he is more suicide-prone in his older years. In fact, the rate of suicide among retired males is exceeded only by the suicide rate of adolescent males.

The research of Hans Selye has given us some insight into how the human system handles physiological and psychological stress. He says that the organism experiences a three-stage excitement, going through cycles of shock followed by resistance and exhaustion. If the stress is not handled adequately it will produce injury to the organism. The process is called the General Adaptation Syndrome.

1. *Shock.* When the body or mind receives a shock, it marshals all of its resources to resist whatever is causing the discomfort. The stimuli may be internal or external, real or imaginary, weak or strong. The system responds all-or-nothing to restore balance to the system.

2. *Resistance.* Resistance follows the initial shock immediately. It is automatic, a part of the reflex function of the central nervous system. The length and severity of the shock will control the amount of resistance and how long it must last. If the shock is not minimized soon enough, the system will experience exhaustion.

3. *Exhaustion.* Prolonged resistance to a shock will exhaust the organism, leading to injury. Selye suggests that "we may estimate the point of maturity to be at the time in life when the General Adaptation Syndrome system becomes less efficient and begins to use up its in-born supply of energy.[8]

Psychological stress that reaches the exhaustion stage and is not relieved will develop both emotional and physiological problems. Such health problems as colitis, peptic or duodenal ulcers, a herniated esophagus, migraines, hypertension, asthma, some forms of arthritis, and cardiac problems are the result of unrelieved stress.

It is important for a man to have regular physical checkups as he ages in order to catch early the problems that are induced by stress as well as other problems of aging, such as diabetes, glaucoma, and prostrate abnormalities.

Social Aging

Social aging is related to social habits compared with the expectations of family, society, and culture on the aging male. The highest incidence of arrests for males over 40 is for drunkenness. Middle-aged men as a whole are more law-abiding than younger men and, when they do break the law, the penalties are not as harsh as they are for younger men. This may be because the crimes of the middle-aged and older adult are more subtle and less violent that the criminal activities of younger males.

Preparing for retirement does not begin at 65 or 70. It must begin in midlife if the process is to be successful. "Adults should contemplate and plan for retirement 10 or even 20 years prior to the actual date of receiving a gold watch and attending the retirement banquet."[9] It has been discovered that a man seldom enjoys a hobby or recreation in his retirement years that he did not at least experiment with in his youth. For that reason, it is essential for young men to examine hobbies and recreations that they will be able to enjoy when they have more time and less vigor than they do at their physical prime. Beyond the contact sports, young men should develop skills in a variety of physical activities that will give them pleasure and help them remain physically fit into their advanced years.

Buhler calls the forties the period of "consolidation" and the late fifties and sixties a period of "evaluation."[10] It is the evaluation process that brings into focus processes of disengagement or "load-shedding," which has four dimensions: "less involvement with other people, a reduction in the variety of social roles played, greater use of mental ability rather than physical activity, and less physical strength to initiate and endure sustained activity."[11]

EXPLORING MATURITY

Maturity has been defined as "the state or condition of complete or adult form, structure, and function of an organism . . . a vaguely defined condition which may refer to (1) practical wisdom in contrast with intelligence; (2) steady and socially acceptable emotional behavior; or (3) mastery of effective social techniques."[12] Christian manhood involves all three of these dimensions and more. It implies the resolution of challenges at each stage of ego development in Erikson's "Eight Ages of Man" and is best illustrated by Maslow's description of the self-actualized person.

The mature man is oriented to the real world, accepts himself and others for what they actually are, and has a high degree of spontaneity. He is problem-centered rather than self-centered, autonomous within himself, and independent, with a fresh appreciation of people and the world. He may be somewhat mystical and identify strongly with his fellowman, displaying an "older-brother" personality. He maintains deep and intimate relationships with only a small circle of friends. He is strongly democratic in his value orientation and understands the difference between means to achieve a goal and the rightful ends to be achieved. He has a good sense of humor that is neither cruel nor sarcastic and has a tremendous capacity to be creative but swims against the mainstream of life and is open to new experiences. As a Christian, the mature man adjusts to the challenges of life as measured by his concept of the kingdom of heaven and the will of God for his life. He is actualizing in Christ, not *in* himself nor *for* himself.

The process is developmental. Havighurst has divided adulthood into three phases and has enumerated tasks that need to be accomplished at each stage. The tasks of the young adult male include "getting started in an occupation, taking on civic responsibility and finding a congenial social group." If he chooses to marry he adds the tasks of "selecting a mate, learning to live with a marriage partner, starting a family, and rearing children." Whether he is single or married, the mature male must maintain a constant relationship with God and find fellowship in a body of believers.

In middle age the man is faced with such tasks as:

1. Achieving adult civic and social responsibility
2. Establishing and maintaining an economic standard of living
3. Assisting teenage children to become responsible and happy adults
4. Developing adult leisure-time activities
5. Relating oneself to one's spouse as a person
6. Accepting and adjusting to psychological changes in middle years
7. Adjusting to aging parents.

To Havighurst's list should be added the necessity for maintaining a personal walk with God and involvement in Christian service.

The developmental tasks of later maturity include:

1. Adjusting to decreasing physical strength and health
2. Adjusting to retirement and reduced income
3. Adjusting to death of spouse
4. Establishing an explicit affiliation with one's age group
5. Meeting social and civic obligations
6. Establishing satisfactory physical living arrangements.[13]

Again, maintaining a personal walk with God and sustaining fellowship with a nurturing body of believers is important to the aging Christian man.

In her book *Coping With Loneliness* Inez Spence tells of her experiences in moving through the developmental tasks of aging, rearing two sons, losing her husband, entering the work force, and then being compelled to retire because of glaucoma. I have known her for 40 years, so have watched it all transpire. Her biggest struggle came when she was forced to retire from her position as dormitory hostess and director of women's activities of a Christian college. When her ophthalmologist told her that retirement was necessary, he talked to her about the processes of adjustment. She couldn't handle it. She came to me with the complaint: "Adjust! Adjust! Adjust! I can't stand the sound of the word." She struggled with the thoughts of retirement and the necessity to adjust. She describes the resolution of the struggle this way:

One night I knelt to pray. Very honestly I told the Lord my true feelings.

"I know, Lord Jesus, what I have to do. My heart is neither questioning nor resentful. The sorrow that You have sent me, I accept. But, please, Lord, give me a substitute word for the word 'adjust.' I cannot explain my feelings concerning it, I can only admit them. Give me something, please, that will be meaningful to me."

Quietly I waited. Long years ago I had learned that God meets the honest heart. Then, softly and clearly, came the words to mind:

"A new assignment in living."

"Thank You, dear Lord," I cried. "Thank You so much. I accept the new assignment. I will not try to hide behind the door that You have shut. I will step out and face, without fear, the new door that You have opened."

And, that day I knew that I had taken a big step in the right direction.[14]

Actually, that is what maturity is all about: adjusting to the new assignments in living. The older we grow, the more adjustments we face. Taking each change as a new assignment in living rather than a disruption from the past can make the transition easier and the outcome more pleasant.

ACHIEVING INTEGRITY

In previous chapters we have examined the "Eight Ages of Man" enumerated by Erikson. The final stage of maturity in his scheme is Integrity Versus Despair. He suggests that the man who is to achieve the ultimate goal of life—integrity—is one who will have learned to handle the previous challenges adequately and will move into the aging years and retirement with a sense of ego identity that is wholesome. He will be able to face his declining years with the resolve that comes with accepting and adjusting to change. If he has not learned flexibility in the previous crisis, he will find himself slipping into despair in old age. It is in the despairing male that the problems of aging are exaggerated and the suicide rate climbs.

The man who has moved into his advanced years with integrity can look back on life and accept his successes and failures. Rather than retreat from what he was and what he has become, the adequate older man remains in touch with the realities of life. He makes the adaptations that are necessary as he disengages from controlling life to sharing responsibility with other people and delegating authority. Although it is not always pleasant, the aging man finds that he can face loss without despair. Someone else moves into his job. He may lose his companion, close up the family home, and move to smaller quarters. The flexibility that has made him successful at the earlier transitions of life will fortify the older male for the last moves that indicate to him and those who love him that life is fleeting. It prepares him for the death of loved ones and, ultimately, for his own demise.

I shall never forget when my father called to inform me that my mother had died suddenly from a stroke. He simply said, "Son, I have bad news. Your mother is in heaven." It was a joint announcement of information and attitude. Grief and loneliness accompanied the experience for my father, but not despair. My parents had shared 50 years together. Dad knew that mother was ready to go to her eternal reward, although he was not prepared to let her go. Yet he could accept her death because of the faith they had shared together. He has now outlived her more than a decade and shows the same integrity today that he did in the trauma of years ago. He has also survived the sorrow of burying his second wife. As a son, I have observed that the loss of a companion is no easier the second time around. It brings the same rush of emotions, followed by grief and loneliness.

Erikson equates integrity with a love for mankind that is far different from the narcissistic self-love of childhood.

> Integrity is the ego's accrued assurance of its proclivity for order and meaning—an emotional integration faithful to the image-bearers of the past and ready to take, and eventually to renounce, leadership in the present. It is the acceptance of one's one and only life cycle and of the people who have become significant to it as something that had to be and that, by necessity, permitted no substitutions. It thus means a new and different love of one's parents, free of the wish that they should have been different, and an acceptance of the fact that one's life is one's own responsibility. It is a sense of comradeship with men and women of distant times and of different pursuits who have created order and objects and sayings conveying human dignity and love. Although aware of the relativity of all the various life styles which have given meaning to human striving, the possessor of integrity is ready to defend the dignity of his own life style against all physical and economic threats. For he knows that an individual life is the accidental co-incidence of but one life cycle with but one segment of history, and that for him all human integrity stands and falls with the one style of integrity of which he partakes.[15]

The integrity of aging does allow flexibility of role changes in the developmental process. I discovered this when my mother died suddenly at age 70. As the only surviving child of my parents, I moved into a new relationship with my father, for he turned to me for strength. I made the funeral arrangements, handled the legal affairs, sold the apartment complex that mother had managed, and moved my father into an apartment near his shoe shop so he could continue working.

As we stood by mother's coffin, Dad said, "Having lived

with your mother for 50 years, there is no other woman I could ever be interested in." I smiled, because mother had frequently said, "Your father will be helpless when I'm gone. Be sure to help him find a good wife."

A month after I moved Dad into his apartment, I returned for a visit. It wasn't long before he said, "What would you think if I brought the landlady up for a visit sometime?" I responded with, "Dad, you have to be careful. We have a reputation in this town. What will the neighbors think?" We both laughed because that was the way he had treated my first ventures into dating when I was a teenager. It was also a serious time as we considered together the factors of dating and courtship in the advanced years.

Having watched my father for more than a half-century as he has moved from young adulthood into retirement gives me an appreciation for what Erikson is saying. I have watched my father demonstrate responsibility for his own behavior, develop and defend his own lifestyle, and disengage from his family of origin while allowing me the same privilege without rupturing either intergenerational relationship. I have watched him retire from his profession but maintain a vigorous physical routine and maintain his health into his eighties.

The aging man who does not develop integrity becomes lost in despair. According to Erikson, this is a condition where:

Fate is not accepted as the frame of life, death not as its finite boundary. Despair expresses the feeling that time is short, too short for the attempt to start another life and to try out alternate roads to integrity. Such a despair is often hidden behind a show of disgust, a misanthrophy, or a chronic contemptuous displeasure with particular institutions and particular people—a disgust and a displeasure which, where not allied with the vision of a superior life, only signify the individual's contempt for himself.[16]

Regret or remorse over lost opportunities compounded by a fear of death plague the aging man who has not explored the upper levels of life's potentials. It shows on his face. It is revealed in his attitudes. And, unfortunately, it leads to a loneliness that compounds his despair.

Every man must face death (Hebrews 9:27). Whether the event will come early in life or late is known only to God. But death is certain. Pleck notes that on the average, men die younger than women.[17]

The life expectancy of men born in the United States in 1975 is 68.7 years compared to 76.5 years for women—a difference of 7.8 years. The difference between men's and women's life expectancies has increased over this century. In 1900, they were 46.3 and 48.3 years, respectively, and differed by only two years.[18]

Pleck continues to note that "the male role is hazardous to men's health in a variety of ways:[19]

1. Aggressiveness and competitiveness cause men to put themselves in dangerous situations.
2. Emotional inexpressiveness causes psychosomatic and other health problems.
3. Men take greater risks.
4. Men's jobs expose them to physical danger.
5. Men's jobs expose them to psychological stress.
6. The male role socializes men to have personality characteristics associated with high mortality (for example, Type A behavior).[20]
7. Responsibilities as family breadwinners expose men to psychological stress.
8. The male role encourages certain specific behavior that endanger health, specifically tobacco-smoking and alcohol consumption.
9. The male role psychologically discourages men from taking adequate medical care of themselves."

Concluding his discussion on why men have a lower life expectancy than women, Pleck observes: "Current research suggests that drinking and smoking may be particularly important factors in men's lower life expectancy.[21] Retherford estimates that half of the current sex differential results from tobacco smoking alone."[22]

The way a person faces the end of his life and the approach of death becomes a barometer of the essence of his life. Plato describes the death of Socrates and quotes his final words: "The time has come for me to go away. I go to die and you to live but which of us goes to the better lot is known to none but God." Compare this with the dying affirmation of the apostle Paul:

> I say this because I won't be around to help you very much longer. My time has almost run out. Very soon now I will be on my way to heaven. I have fought long and hard for my Lord, and through it all I have kept true to him. And now the time has come for me to stop fighting and rest. In heaven a crown is waiting for me which the Lord, the righteous Judge, will give me on that great day of his return. And not just to me, but to all those whose lives show that they are eagerly looking forward to his coming back again (2 Timothy 4:6-8 TLB).

Genesis 49 has an interesting picture of an old man wrapping up his life with integrity. Jacob calls all his sons together and imparts a blessing to each, including the sons of Joseph. "Then, when Jacob had finished his prophecies to his sons, he lay back in the bed, breathed his last, and died" (Genesis 49:33). The serenity of a task completed!

But Christianity involves more than a death to die. It is a life to live. The man who accepts the challenges of life at each stage and handles each task appropriately will find fulfillment at each level. This upward spiral of moving from the cradle to the grave offers a man an opportunity to maximize his potential repeatedly. The more efficient he is in the earlier stages, the easier it will be to handle the later crisis. If he perseveres, the man of God will find that he can approach aging with the ageless attitudes that lead him into the fullness of integrity without the disgust of despair. He will know that he has lived a good life and can face eternity with the anticipation of enjoying the glories of the life yet to come (1 Corinthians 13:12; 1 Thessalonians 4:15-18).

Notes

1. J. E. Birren, ed., *Relations of Development and Aging* (Springfield, IL: Charles C. Thomas, 1964).
2. E. L. Vincent and P. C. Martin, *Human Psychological Development* (New York: Ronald, 1961).
3. Ledford J. Bischof, *Adult Psychology* (New York: Harper and Row, 1969), p. 211.
4. Ibid., p. 224.
5. Charlotte Buhler, "Meaningful Living in the Mature Years," in R. W. Leemeier, ed., *Aging and Leisure* (New York: Oxford, 1961). Jim Conway, *Men in Mid-Life Crisis* (Elgin, IL: David C. Cook Publishers, 1978). Sally Conway, *You and Your Husband's Mid-Life Crisis* (Elgin, IL: David C. Cook Publishers, 1980).
6. Bischof, *Adult Psychology,* p. 226.
7. O. Billig and R. W. Adams, "Emotional Conflicts of the Middle-aged Man," in *Geriatrics,* 1957, vol. 12, pp. 535-41.
8. Hans Selye, *The Stress of Life* (New York: McGraw-Hill, 1956),
9. Bischof, *Adult Psychology,* p. 3.
10. Charlotte Buhler, "Theoretical Observations About Life's Basic Tendencies," in *American Journal of Psychotherapy,* 1959, vol. 13, pp. 561-81.
11. J. E. Birren, *The Psychology of Aging* (Englewood Cliffs, NJ: Prentice-Hall, 1964).
12. English and English, *A Comprehensive Dictionary of Psychological and Psycholanalytical Terms* (New York:

David McKay Company, Inc., 1958).

13. R. J. Havighurst, *Human Development and Education* (New York: McKay, 1953).

14. Inez Spence, *Coping With Loneliness* (Grand Rapids: Baker Book House, 1970), p. 22.

15. Erik H. Erikson, *Identity: Youth and Crisis* (New York: W. W. Norton and Company, Inc., 1968), pp. 139-140.

16. Ibid., p. 140.

17. Joseph H. Pleck, *The Myth of Masculinity* (Cambridge, MA: The MIT Press, 1981), p. 150.

18. J. Harrison, "Warning: The Male Sex Role May Be Hazardous to Your Health," in *Journal of Social Issues,* 35(1):65-86, 1978.

19. Pleck, *Myth,* pp. 150-51.

20. M. Friedman and R. Rosenman, *Type A Behavior and Your Heart* (Greenwich, CT: Fawcett, 1974).

21. Harrison, "Warning," pp. 65-86.

22. R. Retherford, *The Changing Sex Differential in Mortality* (Westport, CT: Greenwood Press), p. 1975.

Chapter 13
Health of Our Whole Man

Why is America presently into the health craze? It's difficult to remember any conversation recently in which diet, exercise, and leisure did *not* come up. The reason we are so preoccupied with health is that we are in fact flabby, out of shape, and overstressed. As we mentioned in Chapter 1, men are especially prone to all kinds of diseases related to stress. Dr. Kenneth Cooper, author of *The New Aerobics,* observes: "Heart disease is a national disaster. Every year nearly a million Americans die from heart and blood vessel disease—a death rate higher than that of any other country!"[1] According to J. Allan Peterson of Family Concern, part of the reason for this kind of statistic comes from the fact that "the average businessman thinks of his body as a machine to be driven to the limit of its endurance, simultaneously pouring into it alcohol, nicotine, pep pills, tranquilizers, and lot of groceries."[2]

The sixties are The Age of Anxiety. The seventies and probably the eighties are Ages of Stress and Depression. We are quickly learning that stress and depression are physically related. Exercise, correct diet, proper rest, and leisure all significantly affect the amounts of stress and depression that a person experiences. In fact, as I do psychotherapy with anxious and depressed people, I emphasize exercise, diet, leisure, and social activities as integral parts of the therapeutic process.

CAUSES OF STRESS AND DEPRESSION

Achievement Stress and the Fear of Failure

We live in a competitive society, especially among men. We've always been taught to win. Our self-esteem has depended upon how many dollars we accumulate, how tough we are, how many women we conquer, how many points we score, how many books we write, how many degrees we earn, and the kind of house and neighborhood we live in. Striving for these goals produces stress. Not accomplishing them generates depression and discouragement.

Sedentary Lifestyles

The average American spends more time with a TV set than in any other activity besides work or sleep. And what about entertainment? Most of it is sedentary: watching movies, plays, football, basketball, tennis, or golf. One study recently concluded that the number one American pastime is eating at a restaurant!

Personality Type

Dr. Meyer Friedman, a cardiologist in San Francisco, divides the male personality into two categories, Type A and Type B.[3] The Type A man, he estimates, runs seven times the risk of coronary heart disease as does the Type B man. Type A is ambitious, aggressive, self-confident, self-demanding, competitive, and driven by the clock. He has an overwhelming need for success. Type B may be as serious as Type A, but he is easier on himself and more patient with other people. He does not carry his job around with him 24 hours a day. During free time Type A may whack a tennis ball or a racquetball around with the same intensity with which he conducts a business meeting. Type B may loaf or read a novel.

Driving through a beautiful mountain canyon, Type A would probably look for the fastest way through and curse at slow semitrucks, attempting desperately to pass them. His heart would be pounding a mile a minute as he worried with almost utter panic whether he would find a motel. Type B, on the other hand, would ride through the same mountain canyon enjoying every moment, taking in the breathtaking view, without giving much thought about the truck in front of him. Type B enjoys the process of experiencing the canyon. Type A can think only of the goal: getting through the canyon to the other side.

Think of it this way: when was the last time you enjoyed the process—the experience of an event—as opposed to the end result—where it would get you? The answer to that question will give you some excellent clues to whether you label yourself "A" or "B." Do you look forward to the orgasm of sex or do you enjoy the process of mutual sexual experience? Do you attend church because it fulfills God's requirements and you'll make some business contacts, or do you take time to be immersed in the experience of worship? Do you take a vacation so your family will be satisfied and so you can tell your neighbor you've been to Hawaii, or do you experience the enjoyment of it moment by moment?

WHAT CAN YOU DO?

Get a Thorough Physical Checkup Every Year

If men are likely to die younger than women, it makes good sense for us to be preventive. When we buy a new automobile, we spend much time and energy keeping the paint job spotless, along with the upholstery and dashboard. We glean the manual to make sure we're changing the oil often enough and that the car is getting the right gas and lubrication. We make an appointment with the local mechanic the minute something doesn't sound right. But what about our bodies? We just let them run without looking under the "hood." If we hear or feel something strange, we tend to cover it up or deny it in hopes that it will go away. We actually treat our cars better than we treat our own bodies!

Exercise

Dr. John C. McCamy and James Presley write in *Human Life Styling:*

> Isolating each risk factor, we find that at age forty a man has five times more chance of giving himself a heart attack if he is overweight. If he does absolutely no exercise, his dangers are six times those of a man who takes a short walk every day. Those who regularly do aerobic exercises—sustained walking, running, swimming, and biking may lower their risks as much as *one hundred times!*[4]

These facts alone should be enough to strongly encourage each of us to engage in physical exercise. In addition, exercise has been shown to be effective in decreasing depression. Vigorous physical activity just three times a week over a four-week period has also been shown to increase energy levels and decrease appetite. We are actually more alert mentally when engaging in a regular exercise regimen.

Before embarking on any vigorous program, contact a cardiologist and allow him to put you through a stress test with an EKG. This involves having you run or walk up and down steps for a period of time and then monitoring the beating pattern of your heart in order to detect irregularities. This step may seem superfluous to you, but people have suffered heart damage by beginning with the wrong kinds and amounts of exercise.

If you refuse to go to a physician there are a couple of telltale signs indicating the state of your cardiovascular system. One, if your resting pulse is more than 80 beats per minute, you are probably in pretty bad shape and under increased risk of coronary heart disease and death in middle age. According to Dr. Lawrence Morehouse, author of *Total Fitness,* the mortality rate for men and women with pulse rates over 92 is four times greater than for those with pulse rates less than 67. He also indicates that irregular heartbeat warrants an immediate evaluation by your physician.

The "weekend athlete" is asking for trouble. Most doctors and other authorities on exercise recommend a half hour of vigorous exercise at least three times per week. Another part of the secret is to begin modestly and work up gradually to more-strenuous exercise. Begin by walking six blocks a day for a week. Then move up to seven blocks. Or begin with 20 minutes of tennis, then 30, then 40.

1. *Make it fun.* A real key to maintaining a fitness program is to do something that is interesting, enjoyable, and fun. If you hate running, play tennis. If exercising alone is boring, find some willing partners to work out with you. It's very important to find a type of recreation that will develop and relax you at the same time. I've found that playing basketball, tennis, or racquetball with a good friend is an excellent way to get rid of tension and enjoy myself at the same time.

Health clubs are popping up all over the place. Sometimes making a long-term commitment to such a facility is the best way to stay disciplined. A few years back Karen and I took out a membership at a local health club. In fact, we enrolled for a lifetime membership! You might be thinking that this is a little extreme. Yet at the time of this writing the cost of a one-year membership is almost as high as the lifetime membership was a few years ago. We needed that kind of commitment to get ourselves off dead center. It's also a neat way to exercise, spending the time with my lover.

2. *Suggested exercise routine.* If you are at a loss as to what might be a desirable and worthwhile regimen, here is a suggestion give by a sports medicine friend of mine. It's very simple, yet helpful in both building strength and conditioning your heart and lungs.

Begin with stretching exercises, *mild stretching.* Take this part very slowly and hold each stretch for 10 to 15 seconds. Only stretch as far as you can without pain. Do as many pushups and situps as you can without straining. Then, on subsequent days, as you feel comfortable, gradually add more repetitions. Don't try to be a superman all at once. Slow progression is the answer. Be patient.

When you've completed your pushups and situps, move into freestyle exercise. This might include one or a few of the following on any given day: bicycling (vigorously), tennis (vigorously), running in place, rope-jumping, jogging, walking briskly, swimming laps, racquetball, handball, competitive basketball, stationary bicycle, walking or running on a treadmill, aerobics exercise class.

If you have questions concerning how long you should engage in any of these activities, buy *The New Aerobics* by Kenneth Cooper.[5] He has charts listing most of these activities and what is appropriate for different age levels. Also, he describes how to progress from smaller to larger quantities of time. At the low level, beginning with 10 minutes of continuous exercise is probably safe. From there you may want to build all the way up to an hour. But, again, do this progressively. And check all this out with a physician before you begin, especially if you are 35 or older and have had any signs of high blood pressure or cardiovascular problems. An exercise regimen like this should be repeated three to four times per week in order to derive any benefits. The weekend athlete may be asking for more trouble than the sedentary nonexerciser.

Diet

So much has been written about diet that one more "sermon" on the topic will doubtless be redundant. However, some psychological principles of dieting may be worthwhile mentioning.

1. *Spread the food out on your plate.* This gives at least the psychological effect that you will be satisfied.

2. *Eat your meals slowly.* Savor each bite by chewing it thoroughly. Some diet experts recommend putting your fork or spoon down between bites. By slowing down you will tend

to be satisfied with less food.

3. *Go grocery shopping when you are full,* not on an empty stomach. The reasons are obvious: those bakery items will be less tempting.

4. *Exercise before mealtime.* Vigorous activity moves blood away from your stomach, leaving you less hungry for the upcoming meal.

5. *Drink water, coffee, or tea about a half hour before mealtime.* Liquids like these will fill your stomach and take the edge off some of your hunger.

6. *Keep low-calorie snacks around,* such as carrot sticks, celery, and cauliflower, as opposed to corn chips or doughnuts.

7. *Allow yourself to eat only at the kitchen table.* This will limit the stimuli which surround food intake. Forbid yourself from eating while watching television or lounging on the back patio.

8. *Cut the boredom in your life.* Eating is often a substitute for fun and enjoyment.

9. *Eat dessert occasionally.* But settle for a small portion, and savor every bite.

10. *Don't give up when you blow it.* One of the leading reasons that people give up on reasonable dieting is the aftermath of gorging. The person says to himself, "What's the use? I may as well eat and eat and give up my diet. I'll never make it anyway." No! Just put yourself back on the principles of dieting. Ask yourself, "How can I resist more successfully next time?"

Notes

1. Kenneth Cooper, M.D., *The New Aerobics* (New York: Bantam Books, 1970).

2. J. Allan Peterson, *For Men Only* (Wheaton: Tyndale, 1973).

3. M. Friedman and R. Rosenman, *Type A Behavior and*

Your Heart (Greenwich, CT: Fawcett, 1974).

4. John C. McCamy and James Presley, *Human Life Styling* (New York: Harper and Row, 1975).

5. Kenneth Cooper, M.D., *The New Aerobics* (New York: Bantam Books, 1970).

Chapter 14
Jesus: The Perfect Man

Our model of manhood is Jesus Christ. Though He was God incarnate, He was also truly human. Yet He lived a style of relating above reproach. His lifestyle is our ultimate goal. We may not be able to model His life in its ultimate form, but by looking at the way He moved through life we can catch glimpses of what we are called to be. Many of these glimpses will reiterate principles of relating and living that we have discussed in previous chapters. Hopefully this summary will solidify these principles and make them even more understandable to you.

In his very helpful book *Training Christians to Counsel,* H. Norman Wright outlines Jesus' style of relating. Let's look at this style in some detail.[1]

JESUS WAS OBEDIENT TO GOD HIS FATHER

In the Garden of Gethsemane Jesus struggled with His own will versus the Father's will. We are told that "sweat dropped to the ground like drops of blood" while Jesus anguished over His upcoming plight. Does this sound familiar? Yet He finally responded by saying, "Not my will but thine be done." In my own life when I have tried too hard to control outcomes, goals, and the future myself, I have often ended up falling over my own trappings. I need to realize that I am human, and this means that I can go only so far in planning and controlling my environment. There has to be a point where I finally say, "Lord, I've done all I know how to do; the rest is up to You." Keith Miller suggests this same idea very succinctly in *The Edge of Adventure.* He suggests that your last request in daily prayer time be, "And as for me, Lord, Your will be done in my life."[2]

Since I have been finishing my prayer time with that desire, all kinds of blessings have come forth in my life, and I have learned to let go of some of the selfish control and over-concern that I have developed through the years. "Let go, let God." "The Lord only wants you to do what you can do, and He will take over from there." Are these true statements? In Proverbs 16:9 we are told, "We should make plans —counting on God to direct us" (TLB). Isaiah 58:11 states, "The Lord will continually guide you" (NASB). "The Lord is the one who goes ahead of you; He will be with you. He will not fail you or forsake you. Do not fear or be dismayed" (Deuteronomy 31:8 NASB). And finally, "Commit everything you do to the Lord. Trust him to help you do it and he will" (Psalm 37:5 TLB).

JESUS LIVED A LIFE OF FAITH

At a seminar I attended recently one of the speakers stated that to "*act in faith* is to say: because of a particular truth, I will act in a particular manner." In a sense, to act in faith is to be willing to give up my selfish rights to do what is best. Jesus experienced all of man's ups and downs, temptations and human dilemmas. He acted in faith because He was willing to become truly man.

It takes a *real* man to act in faith because of a particular truth. If we are exhorted in James 1:19 to be a ready listener, what do we do? As a father, do I assume the role of "head of the house" by telling my kids how high to jump and when? Or do I listen to their feelings and experiences? As a husband, do I fall asleep while my wife is describing some feelings which are cutting her to the core? As a friend, do I glance nervously at my watch and out the window as my business associate describes his feelings of loneliness and marital disillusionment? Jesus acted on principles of truth. Do you?

JESUS' PRAYER LIFE

The example of Jesus' prayer life indicates that prayer is a very important element in living out our faith. In Luke 5:16 it is recorded that Jesus "withdrew himself into the wilderness, and prayed." Apparently this was a solitary experience. Recently I walked around a section of Karen's dad's farm in Iowa as part of my own aerobics-exercise program. It was a four-mile walk, so I had about an hour to myself. I decided to spend the entire time in prayer to the Lord. This solitary time with Him was one of the most exciting, real interactions I've had with God in a long time. The only "ears" available to hear me as I conversed out loud to my heavenly Father were on the cornstalks. It was a beautiful time of "walking in God's light" and feeling His presence in a tangible way.

When is the last time you spent *15 minutes* with God alone —just you and Him? At a recent men's retreat one of my friends suggested that we spend 15 minutes at the end of the seminar to ponder with God the meaning of what had been said for our lives. During that short period most of the men were tearful, including my friend and myself. These 15 minutes alone with God were the most meaningful moments spent during the entire men's retreat. Apparently our prayer life with the Lord is important!

Apparently it is also critical to pray when we have an important decision to make. "And it came to pass in those days that he went out into a mountain to pray, and continued all night in prayer to God. And when it was day, he called unto him his disciples; and of them he chose twelve, whom also he named apostles" (Luke 6:12,13). Here was God Incarnate, who was all-knowing, praying through the night to His Father for guidance in making decisions concerning who would be His apostles. He was modeling for us what our response is to be in the face of decision. If Jesus prayed for hours in order to determine His actions for the next day, what should our response be to similar life situations?

JESUS' PERSONAL INVOLVEMENT WITH PEOPLE

Jesus was not aloof. He was personal. He was sensitive. He was caring. Jesus was a man of compassion, experiencing sorrow for the suffering of other individuals. We see this expressed in Mark 8:2: "I have compassion on the multitude, because they have now been with me three days and have nothing to eat." Mark 1:40,41: "Then a leper came to Jesus, knelt in front of him and appealed to him, 'If you want to, you can make me clean.' Jesus was filled with pity for him, and stretched out his hand and placed it on the leper, saying, 'Of course I want to—*be clean!*' " (Phillips). Mark 6:34; "And Jesus, when he came out, saw many people, and was moved with compassion toward them, because they were as sheep not having a shepherd; and he began to teach them many things."

In my consulting office I have met with countless men who have shed tears of compassion and empathy for their children, wives, and friends but choke back these same tears with a great force of energy when in the proximity of their loved ones. Why? How is it that a 6-foot, 180-pound male is frightened to death of shedding tears in the vicinity of a 5-foot, 120-pound female or an even smaller youngster? One of the best legacies my own father has given me has been his ability to shed tears over the death of a friend or the tragedy of neighbors. I hope I have the courage to pass this same legacy on to my two sons. Jesus wept; and was He a man!

JESUS ACCEPTED OTHERS

The thief hanging beside Jesus on his own cross was accepted by Jesus. There was not evidence of condemnation coming from Jesus even as He faced the pain and frustration of dying. In John 4 Jesus spends one of His longest conversations recorded in the New Testament not only with one of the despised Samaritans, but with a Samaritan woman of disrepute, who had had five husbands!

John 8:7 NIV depicts a model of acceptance for us as well: "If any one of you is without sin, let him be the first to throw a stone at her." He is saying, in effect, that a man's first response to someone who has missed the mark is to *accept,* not condemn. He gives this woman another chance. As a man, what is your response to your teenage daughter who breaks curfew? Does she receive a five-minute lecture on morality and the sins of lustful living? Or do you convey the attitude that Jesus portrayed in this passage: "I do not condemn you, but do not sin again."? Jesus, who had all the self-righteous prerogative in the world to condemn this woman, basically said, "You blew it, no doubt about it, but I'm not going to condemn you for it. I don't want you to continue blowing it, however. I'd appreciate it if you'd stop messing around!" I once heard a speaker say, "A person cannot grow unless he is accepted." Jesus first accepted people where they were, without condemnation. Then He told them what His will for their lives was. Jesus knew the psychology of conviction and learning. First accept, then instruct.

JESUS GAVE WORTH TO THE INDIVIDUAL

Jesus spent lots of time walking, talking, and sharing with His disciples. Instead of conversing with Zacchaeus, the chief tax collector, on the street and on the run, Jesus went to Zacchaeus's house and dined with him and his family while they talked together. Christ gave credence to Peter, His egocentric disciple, by washing his feet. Washing a man's feet was the most humble act a man could perform for another person in those days.

Urie Bronfenbrenner, a giant in the area of child psychology, relates an incident in which a man worked nights for a month as a taxi driver in order to make enough money to buy his children expensive Christmas presents. The father's intent, I'm sure, was to impart his love for his children through this sacrifice of time. Bronfenbrenner comments on the sadness of a society that encourages a man to impart worth through dollars and the material. What if that same father had spent that same 160 hours with his children, listening to their dreams, walking with them, and sharing his own joys, fears, hopes, and dreams? What imparts a real sense of self-worth to another struggling human? Our Lord knew the secret, didn't He?

JESUS REQUIRED ACCEPTING RESPONSIBILITY

Jesus gave worth to individuals by allowing them to accept responsibility for their own lives. His parable of the prodigal son is a beautiful example of this principle. The father did not condemn the wayward son but instead allowed him to experience the logical consequences of his own actions.

Jesus did not tell the woman at the well to go back to her first husband, nor did He tell her what to do. He merely confronted her with the facts: "You have had five husbands . . . I am the Christ." And the woman drew her own conclusions, spreading the good news among the Samaritans. Christ Jesus confronts us with the facts and leaves the choices up to us. He treats us like adults.

As men, I believe that we are called to bring our family members back to the principles of truth outlined in the Word of God. We do this through forming a close relationship with family members, giving worth to each individual, and confronting in love by inviting others to explore the ways in which they fall short. In order to be most effective through confronting in this way, a man must be willing to admit his own mistakes and be a model of serving God's purposes. We are reminded in Proverbs 28:13, "A man who refuses to admit his mistakes can never be successful" (TLB). Confronting in love means *inviting* other people to explore their possible shortcomings. There is no way you can force someone to think about growth, but you can extend an invitation. "Have you thought about this?" "What would happen if . . . ?" "I would really appreciate it if . . ."

JESUS GAVE HOPE, ENCOURAGEMENT, AND INSPIRATION

Jesus moved through life positively. He saw and gave hope to people wherever He traveled. Mark 10:26,27: "And they were astonished out of measure, saying among themselves, Who then can be saved? And Jesus, looking upon them, said, With men it is impossible, but not with God; for with God all things are possible." Matthew 11:28: "Come unto me, all ye that labor and are heavy laden, and I will give you rest." John 14:27: "Peace I leave with you; my peace I give unto you; not as the world giveth, give I unto you. Let not your heart be troubled, neither let it be afraid."

Notice the language in these passages. Jesus is not saying, "For with God *some* things *may be* possible." No, He does not speak as a tentative philosopher or a theologian asking ultimate questions about life. He states instead, "With God *all* things *are* possible." He is absolutely certain about what He is saying. That absolute certainty in His message gives us a real hope and a solid encouragement.

We even have a hope in the face of death:
Lo! I tell you a mystery. We shall not all sleep, but we shall all be changed, in a moment, in the twinkling of an eye. . . . For the trumpet will sound, and the dead will be raised imperishable, and we shall be changed. For this perishable nature must put on the imperishable, and this mortal nature must put on immortality . . . then shall come to pass the saying that is written:

"Death is swallowed up in victory."
"O death, where is thy victory?
O death, where is thy sting?"

. . . Thanks be to God, who gives the victory through our Lord Jesus Christ (1 Corinthians 15:51-57 RSV).

Maxie Dunnam, in his inspiring book *Barefoot Days of the Soul,* expands on this idea:

Resurrection is at the heart of the Christian faith. There's a great big beautiful tomorrow for those who trust Christ and commit themselves to his Lordship. Death has no sting—there is no victory for death in the lives of those who have accepted the gift of eternal life, who have experienced salvation and have become friends of God.[3]

And this promise applies not only to tomorrow; it applies to today. Right now. At this very moment. You may be trapped in a very real "prison experience." You may be saying, "What's the use? What's life all about? What difference does it all make? Isn't life just a big miserable joke?" Yes, it is likely that without Christ life can be interpreted as basically 70 years of ups and downs. But put in the perspective of resurrection, we have hope, celebration of life, and anticipation of a real direction and meaning. We have a goal—to become like Christ. We probably won't reach this goal here on earth, but we have a *promise*—that we will be made whole.

JESUS HELPED TO RESHAPE PEOPLE'S THINKING

Jesus helps us redirect our attention from the unimportant things of life to the important. In the face of discouragement and guilt God offers forgiveness: "*Everyone* who takes refuge in him will be freely pardoned" (Psalm 34:22 TLB).

Jesus said in effect to His fretful and scared disciples, "Don't worry—as long as I'm in the boat it will *never* sink. It may get tossed around by the storm, but it will *never* sink."

The purpose of Christ's message is to get us *thinking* and behaving in more constructive ways. My physiology colleagues tell me that sensations from our eyes, ears, nose, and skin enter the higher centers (thinking, logical parts) of the brain *before* reaching the emotional centers. If that's true, then we think before we feel or act. First there are perceptions which are interpreted in the thinking centers before these same perceptions are allowed to be transferred to the emotional centers.

As Epictetus said: "Men are not worried by things, but by their ideas about things. When we meet with difficulties, become anxious and troubled, let us not blame others, but rather ourselves." What do you think about? H. Norman Wright, in a helpful book titled *Improving Your Self-Image,* states: "As we build storehouses of memories, knowledge, and experience we seem to retain and remember those things which we concentrate upon the most. If we concentrate upon rejection and hurt, they will be a part of our experience. Each person is responsible for the things he allows his mind to dwell upon."[4]

In Ephesians 4:23 we are told, "Now your attitudes and thoughts must all be constantly changing for the better" (TLB). This is to be a continuing experience. Paul said in Romans 12:2, "And do not be conformed to this world, but be transformed by the renewing of your mind" (NASB). The word "renewal" here means "to make new from above." This implies that our thought life can be renovated through prayer, searching God's Word, and believing in the working of the Holy Spirit.[5]

Finally, Paul lays the clincher on us. In Philippians 2:5 he directs us, "Let this mind be in you, which was also in Christ Jesus." The major point here is clear: we are to reflect in our own minds the perspective and imagination of Jesus Christ. What do you suppose He thought about which led Him to right behavior?

JESUS WAS A TEACHER

Jesus taught through the model of His life, through direct statements, and through well-timed questions. We have already discussed in some detail Jesus as a model. He also instructed directly through verbal statements, such as in Luke 5:41,42 in speaking about individual responsibility: "And why quibble about the speck in someone else's eye—his little fault—when a board is in your own? How can you think of saying to him, 'Brother, let me help you get rid of that speck in your eye,' when you can't see past the board in yours? Hypocrite! First get rid of the board, and then perhaps you can see well enough to deal with his speck!'' (TLB).

As men we are to be teachers not only by our example but also through our verbal instruction, as Jesus was doing here. In Deuteronomy 6:6,7 we are told by Moses, "And you must think constantly about these commandments I am giving you today. You must teach them to your children and talk about them when you are at home or out for a walk; at bedtime and the first thing in the morning" (TLB). In other words, as men we are to use every opportunity to instruct our children to be doers of the truth.

If you are a father, don't miss bedtime as a chance to listen to and instruct your children. As often as possible, put your kids to bed or share in that time with your wife. And don't rush through it so you can rush downstairs to the family room to watch TV. Savor those moments. Listen. Take time to apply Christian principles to what has happened that day in the family. Perhaps your child has followed some Christian principle by his actions. Or maybe mom has, or even you. Talk about this in a positive way. Or perhaps some un-Christian principles have been modeled by you or someone else. Talk about this and again discuss briefly some positive alternative responses. Allow your kids to come up with some of these ideas.

Use well-timed questions in your instruction. Jesus did. In Luke 14:2-6, instead of Jesus telling the Pharisees where to get off, He merely asked the question and left the responsibility of answering to each individual present. Each person would have to answer for himself. So often with our teenagers we make the mistake of teaching through laying down rules and pushing our values on them. Many times a well-timed question will be much more instructive. So instead of saying, "If you continue to stay out late, you'll just turn into a bum," perhaps a question would be more instructive: "How is staying out late helping you?" or "How late do you think is reasonable for you to stay out?"

As our children become older we need to encourage them to think through their own decisions. Not that we stop setting limits! But increasingly we as parents help them learn through grappling with life's questions and decision. That's what Jesus did. He asked questions which led people to arrive at responsible answers.

JESUS WAS ASSERTIVE, STRAIGHTFORWARD, AND HONEST

As Christians we are told to grow up "speaking the truth in love" (Ephesians 4:15). Ephesians 4:25 says, "Therefore, rejecting all falsity and done now with it, let everyone express the truth with his neighbor, for we are all parts of one body and members one of another" (Amplified). Looking through a large number of recent books on assertiveness, I could not find a better definition of the term: Assertive people communicate honestly. They are positive in their relations with others, and they take responsibility for themselves. Such persons stand up for their own rights without ignoring the rights of others.

The best example we have of the assertive life is that of Jesus. Read about His straightforwardness with His friends in the Garden of Gethsemane (Luke 22:46) or His candor with the Pharisees (Luke 20) and Zacchaeus (Luke 19:5). When He called His disciples, Jesus did not say, "Come on, you unfortunate slobs, consider yourselves lucky to follow such a leader as I am." That would have been an aggressive response, the kind of remark that I've heard in other forms in today's business world. He also did not coax them to follow Him by beating around the bush. Can you imagine Him saying, "Do you think you could consider following Me for just a few hours?"

No, Jesus was not a passive person. He was direct, yet not

202 / The Emotional Side of Men

abusive. He took the guesswork out of communication by stating straightforwardly, "Come, follow me!" (Mark 1:17 TLB). He asked men to be His followers in an honest, positive manner. If they refused, that was their choice. And if they accepted, they knew exactly what they were saying yes to.

Recently I have been struggling with how to share my own personal faith with other people. Jesus' example is helpful in my endeavor. If we are to be real men, we need to be assertive, straightforward, honest, and genuine in the sharing of ourselves and the meaning that Christ has in our lives. This does not mean jamming the Bible down someone else's throat, but the attitude, "If you really want to know what makes me tick, I'll tell you what my experience has been."

JESUS WAS ANDROGENOUS

Jesus was sensitive and warm. He had compassion for others. He wept. Would these be regarded as feminine characteristics? He also spoke with authority and assertiveness. He became openly angry. He helped people with their logical thinking. Aren't these some of our commonly accepted masculine characteristics? Christ was a person and human. That's what we are called to be—humans, both male and female. A man is not a sissy if he exhibits "feminine characteristics." He is a person in Christ Jesus. Let's be free to be persons in God's image.

Notes

1. H. Norman Wright, *Training Christians to Counsel* (Denver: Christian Marriage Enrichment, 1977).
2. Keith Miller and Bruce Larson, *The Edge of Adventure* (Waco: Word Publishers, 1973).
3. Maxie Dunnam, *Barefoot Days of the Soul* (Waco: Word Books, 1975).

4. H. Norman Wright, *Improving Your Self-Image* (Eugene, OR: Harvest House, 1977).
5. Jerry A. Schmidt, *New Beginnings* (Eugene, OR: Harvest House, 1978).

Epilogue

In this book we have tried to examine masculinity from different aspects. We have tried to show how to avoid the traps of loneliness, perfectionism, and competition by developing meaningful relationships, becoming an adequate person, and living out God's forgiveness. We have examined how to experience and express emotions and have considered the roles of a man a person, husband, father, and worker. Ways to approach aging and to maintain good health habits were also examined. Then we looked at the life of Jesus to see how He set the perfect example of what a man of God should be.

To be like Jesus in the closing decades of this century is not an impossible task. Rather, it is what Christian manhood is all about. We recognize that the process is a spiritual one, but we also know that it involves the totality of being a man: influencing the physical, emotional, and social dimensions of his life.

We offer a closing prayer that we believe v . . help men to be men. It is in three parts. We encourage each man who reads this book to write this prayer on index cards and to post them in various places where he will be reminded to pray the prayer twice a day—morning and evening—in connection with his times of Bible reading. Experience has shown that if a man will sincerely pray this prayer faithfully for 60 days, dramatic changes will occur in his life.

1. *Lord, show me myself as You see me.* This will permit God to show you the good things in your personality and life that He wants to strengthen and develop. It also will permit

Him to show you things that are inappropriate to being a man of God. It will reveal to you some things about yourself that you need to allow the Holy Spirit to change, either to deliver you from them or to refashion you to conform more to His image.

2. *Give me a glimpse of what I could become if I made You Lord and Master of my life.* This is an appeal for a vision, a flash of insight into what God's ultimate goal for your life might be. It opens your mind to receive an inspiration from God to help you set both short-range and long-range goals and to allow His Spirit to lead you in life-changing decisions and behaviors.

3. *Teach me the graces and disciplines to become the man You want me to become.* This request for guidance will allow God's Word to come alive to you and show you how to think and feel about your situation in life and how to respond to what is happening to you.

You will note, as you continue to pray this prayer consistently, that your attitudes and behaviors will begin to change, almost imperceptively, helping you become more like the Biblical presentation of Christ. Other people will probably begin to notice the subtle changes before you do because spiritual growth is usually gradual and more open to objective observation than subjective experience. But the changes will occur because the prayer is consistent with God's revealed Word. If you ask the Holy Spirit, He will help you pray the prayer sincerely.

God bless you as you become the man that God wants you to become!

DATE DUE

261-2500			Printed in USA